A CHAMPION'S MINDSET

THE FIGHTER WITHIN

CHAD GEORGE

CONTENTS

For Logan & Luca

ABOUT THE AUTHOR

CHAD GEORGE is a retired Mixed Martial Arts fighter with over twenty-six professional fights to his name, a Brazilian Jiu-Jitsu Black Belt, and was the first-ever Combat Jiu-Jitsu World Champion. George is considered a pioneer of the lighter-weight divisions in MMA. He has earned considerable respect within the martial arts community, not only for his accolades earned across his fifteen active years of competition but for his ability to build a champion's mindset in others. From fighting on the world's biggest stages to becoming a father, he has always shared the struggles of his journey, past and present, which have been showcased in his two documentary films: Occupation Fighter and The Journey. Chad has become a sought-after coach for some of the top athletes in combat sports and continues to share his story with colleagues, entrepreneurs, and artists worldwide.

PROLOGUE: WHAT IS FIGHTING?

When most people hear the word 'fighting,' they assume it's referring to a threatening and spontaneous physical altercation. However, given the rise in popularity of combat sports, someone today may think about boxing or Mixed Martial Arts instead. So, the meaning of 'fighting' isn't set in stone. What if that means the whole concept of a 'fighter' is much more powerful than we originally thought?

Fighting is in our DNA. Since the dawn of time, humans have been fighting for survival. Even today, we have an innate lust for battle. We are intrigued by the primal instincts of wild animals. We watch movies with epic fight scenes. We throw punches in the air after watching an exciting prize fight.

Everyone has that inner desire to fight, even if they like to pretend they don't. Some fight their fears, others fight the hurdles that cross their path, and then there are those who stand tall in the ring. The desire to fight is inescapable. It lives within all of us, embedded in our genes. We sometimes feel our blood pressure rise and put ourselves in a fantasy dream state where we are a champion. Then reality sets in, and it's back to our normal lives. Back to feeling all the stress and worry when we return to the regrets of our past failures.

When examined closely, we can see that even the seemingly routine days are an example of the great human fighting spirit. We chose to get up in the morning, we chose to go to work, we chose to move forward, and we chose to thrive on. Every day we strive to become better versions of ourselves and continue the fight for a brighter future.

All of us have experienced failure and painful losses. Retired professional Mixed Martial Artist Chad George is no different. Growing up in a small town, Chad was bullied for most of his younger years and was weighed down by limiting beliefs which were reinforced by others. They told him that he wasn't good enough. As a result, he developed a lack of confidence and low self-esteem.

After finally building the courage to leave his hometown, Chad continued to fail. Again and again. He dropped out of college during his senior year. He was humiliated on national television. He wound up homeless, broke, and was told by doctors after major surgery that he would not be able to continue his career as an MMA fighter.

Each time he failed, he wanted to give up. Yet, something drove him to keep going. It was an inexplicable feeling, an unrelenting desire to keep fighting forward.

This is Chad's story – an inspiring glimpse into the raw and emotional journey of an athlete whose struggle through self-development helped mold him into becoming the unbreakable champion he is today.

In Chad's eyes, we are all fighting to become the best versions of ourselves. The idea of a FIGHTER is something that burns within each and every one of us. We all have things to fight for, even if we don't realize it.

A Champion's Mindset was written as a life-changing guide to show that being a champion is a choice. Chad explains discipline, risk, fear, and embracing the unknown. It's our excuses that hold us back. They are the real monster in the mirror. If you want to achieve your dreams and goals, you can. You're just going to have to FIGHT for them.

Chad "Savage" George was born and raised in Sacramento, California. He started his career with wrestling at the age of eleven. In the year 2000, he successfully became a U.S. All-American while attending high school. At age twenty-two, he moved to Los Angeles to pursue an education and career in film and animation. At the time, Mixed Martial Arts (MMA) was still in its infancy. In fact, it was still illegal in California. It was Chad's passion for art that served as the driving force behind his career. Martial arts was not even a thought. Today, he has over fifteen years of active professional competition and twenty-six professional fights under his belt. He has fought all over the world and for some of the largest organizations that exist, including the WEC (Now the UFC) and Bellator.

After a widely successful documentary about Chad's life released in 2012—*Occupation Fighter*—his passion for growth and development only grew stronger. Today, he holds a black belt in Brazilian Jiu-Jitsu, is the first ever Combat Jiu-Jitsu world champion, and has been recognized not only as a pioneer of the Bantamweight division in Mixed Martial Arts but also as one of the top submission artists in the world.

This book contains the full, raw story of Chad George— every heart-stopping drop, unexpected turn, and blind leap of faith. And if you find the fight within yourself to experience the essence of his journey, you will find the champion within yourself, too.

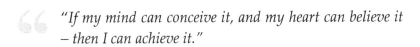

"If my mind can conceive it, and my heart can believe it – then I can achieve it."

— *MUHAMMAD ALI*

1

INTRODUCTION

W hen I first came up with the idea of writing a book, my initial thought was, *"Who the hell am I to write a book?!"* After all, I have absolutely no related experience. In fact, I have always been quite bad at writing. Not only that, but my career and life have seen more ups and downs than a playground see-saw.

People have been telling me that my experiences are inspirational and should be shared with the world. My colleagues kept pushing me to write a book, but I never took it seriously. Then one day, I read a simple quote that changed everything.

 "There comes a point in your life when you need to stop reading other people's books and start writing your own"

— **ALBERT EINSTEIN**

* * *

I felt my story was something that could resonate with anyone. Each one of us has our own battles to fight. We are all unique, but that is one thing we have in common. Everyone has some sort of internal struggle that only they can understand; not everything can be put into words. I have had emotional breakdowns, been embarrassed, experienced crippling self-doubt, been homeless, gone through career changes, suffered heartbreak, and been plagued with insecurities throughout my life.

Looking back at all this, I asked myself a question, "If I have been through so much—and since almost everyone can relate to me in one way or another—then what makes me incapable of writing my story?"

Nothing.

My story is that of someone who refused to accept a life defined by coming up short. It is a journey of constant struggle. A rickety old roller coaster ride with brakes that fail.

In this book, I talk about my struggles and how fighting has allowed me to understand that we are all connected, that we traverse the same roads along this journey called Life. Our routes may differ, as might our destinations, but we all take the same roads to travel, more or less. We all make our own life choices, decide who we want to be as people, and define our own destinies. We will be tested through the rounds of life, time and time again, by questions we don't have the answers to and obstacles we can't overcome. With each battle that we endure—no matter how bloodied and bruised they may leave us—we emerge as much bigger, much stronger monsters.

My goal with this book is to provide you the tools to FIGHT for the life you have always wanted. It's time you wake up the champion that lives within you. I would be lying if I said that my purpose was just to share the information that I and so many others have "woken up" with. This isn't your typical motivational book. Seeing others succeed is what fuels me, and I know there are so many others like me who need to see success stories without any sugar coating. When I speak about my story, I am reminded of my "WHY."

My passion for self-development would be better described as pure obsession. I am obsessed with the process of progression and becoming an increasingly better version of myself. Burning deep within me is the desire to move forward. It keeps me awake at night. It tugs at me in the morning, and like an annoying sibling, it yells at me constantly throughout the day. I cannot escape it. I need to follow it. The chase is real.

 "Don't bend; don't water it down; don't try to make it logical; don't edit your own soul according to the fashion. Rather, follow your most intense obsessions mercilessly."

— FRANZ KAFKA

* * *

I know that there is a champion in every single one of us. At some point, I realized that my WHY is to help others overcome the same struggles that I have battled with my entire life. I know that being a fighter is not my only purpose in life. I have to be a candle to light up the way for so many other people out there. I know this is the time, and so here I am, looking back over my shoulder to illuminate the same path I have trudged so that others can follow.

My journey through professional MMA has provided me with a unique ability to express ideas and to bring light to the notion that WE ALL ARE FIGHTING FOR SOMETHING. You could be fighting for your own self-respect, family, financial stability, or even just self-development. Others may be battling the conflicts of the world, taking on economic crises, or—in my case—prize fighting. Our struggles are miles apart from those of others, yet each of our battles has within it reasons to celebrate.

I'm here to tell you that it's time to stop with the excuses. Excuses have never won a single battle. Stop coming up with reasons why others can and you cannot. The word 'cannot' should be deleted from your vocabulary. If you haven't done that yet, do it now.

 "Ninety-nine percent of the failures come from people who have the habit of making excuses."

— GEORGE WASHINGTON CARVER

It's time to pick yourself up off the floor, dust yourself off, and ditch that doubt. You're not a failure. There will always be times when you won't succeed, but remember one thing— failures are stepping stones to success. I don't care how bad it hurts. The more pain you have been through, the more fulfilling and satisfying the inevitable victory will be. When I was younger, my biggest fear was not being accepted. Now I think to myself, who did I want to be accepted by? Had I accepted myself the way I was, who would've had the guts to walk over me? My self-doubt and lack of confidence was a beacon for many to see the obstacles I faced as an adolescent. From being bullied, to never thinking of myself as good enough. Those are just a couple of the struggles I experienced. But you know what? I am the best I can be today, and tomorrow I will be better than today because I believe in myself. And that's all I need.

To be honest, the memories of my past still haunt me. I don't think they will ever go away. And in some ways, I am glad of that because, although I am a completely different person now, my passion is derived from those experiences. I fight for everything I have today all the more fiercely because of them and refuse to let the past ruin anything ever again.

There will be days when the sun will not shine enough to lighten your path. Hard times will arise, and you must grasp the rope of faith in that darkness. You might not feel like getting out of bed or taking the next big step for yourself, but it is those days that force champions to make a choice—either believe in yourself and push harder than usual or don't. Only a few people understand what this decision really means. And if you are one of them, consider yourself lucky. It is a skill, a single-minded focus, and a dogged degree of determination that doesn't come to you as an inherited trait. It is worked for. You need to learn to hold yourself accountable, and I don't think many of us set the necessary conditions up for ourselves to do that.

Fighting has taught me that the strength I needed was inside me the entire time. I now know that if you believe in yourself, then absolutely anything and everything is possible. Sure, you're going to have to eat some shit. And go through some pain.

That is the key to success. Whenever you get knocked down, get up again and keep going. Every time you fall and pick yourself up again, I bet you will find yourself stronger than before. Your fears will fade away, and your strength will help you stand taller in the face of adversity.

I don't share my stories to make you feel sorry for me. I don't want handouts, and I don't want pity. What I do want is to show you that everyone has their own battles, no matter how things may appear on the surface. Even when the sea appears calm, there are ferocious riptides and sharks hunting their prey below.

My struggles are bound to be different from yours, and yours are surely going to differ from those of the next person. However, what connects us is the idea that we ALL need to fight to prosper. It doesn't require one to be part of a specific gender, race, or religion to succeed. All it takes is a fighter who is bold enough to rise up and smile in the face of adversity. We all need to be that fighter, to stand tall and stare down all the battles of life if we want more out of it. If I can do it, so can you.

It's time to act like a champion.
It's time to breathe like a champion.
It's time to speak like a champion.
It's time to live life like a champion.

Over the years, I've worked with CEOs of Fortune five hundred companies. I have worked with the military, law enforcement, athletes, and people on every level. Each person has always had their unique reasons for needing training. But one thing that has always stood out to me is that they ALL had stories of things they needed to overcome. Struggling is universal.

We see successful people riding in their fancy cars, luxuriating in lifestyles we can only dream of, but do we try to learn where they came from to get there? Many had normal lives like me and you at one point; their success wasn't inherited, but they climbed the ladder that we often ignore.

Throughout all my years of experience, I have learned that no matter what we think someone's appearance may say about them, the truth of their story is so often radically different. We tend to only read the headlines. We believe the hype; we don't hear of the struggle. We don't see the fear. However, we all have it. It's innate, and it stays there, deep inside.

My goal is to develop the strength required to face those primal feelings. I want to let you know that you are not alone. Anyone who is successful today has achieved their greatness through seizing victory from the jaws of setbacks they faced.

Regardless of what stage of life we are in, there will always be something that seems to do its best to tear us down. And I don't think there's anything wrong with that. I think that's what life is supposed to be like. All the ups and downs are what keep us alive… I'm sure we all know what a straight line on an EKG means! The struggles we experience when we are kids drastically differ from the ones we face today, just as the ones we have today will differ from the ones we go through a decade from now.

Every struggle is unique and will need to be taken care of with devotion and persistence. To accomplish this, we need to look at our own inner demons and face the truths they represent. The stuff that is buried deep down. You know the stuff I'm talking about. The stuff we don't want to address is exactly the stuff we need to look at. That is where true power is developed.

I tell every athlete I work with, *"It's when you're tired and don't want to be there. It's when it is no longer fun, and your body hurts. This is where your truth will be visible. How bad do you want it, and how far are you TRULY willing to go?"*

This moment, right here, is the one that matters the most. This is the point where you either decide to be a champion or make an excuse for why you shouldn't move any further. Being a champion is a choice that is completely yours. This is the connection to everything in life. So, how bad do you really want it?

I hope my story will provide you enough insight to come to the realization that anything is possible. If you grind off all your bullshit and allow yourself to develop a champion's mindset, you can turn your life upside down and make your dreams come true.

2

BEING A CHAMPION IS A CHOICE

L ife is a stage on which we are all actors performing our roles. One day you might be recognized as the greatest of all time, and the next, you might be criticized for being done and washed up. It is going to be that way for each one of us. Life is going to hit us all, and—for many—it's going to hit harder than others.

As a kid, I remember watching Mike Tyson on TV with my dad. At the time, he was a monster. The most feared boxer the sport had ever seen. Each time he would fight, it was a big ordeal. Friends came over, we ordered pizza, and made betting games to predict what round a knockout would happen. Watching him fight was something special. Nothing was going to hit you as hard as Mike; except life.

THE PROCESS

When I say the word 'champion,' I am not referring to the ones who've had it easy. Champions are the ones who picked themselves up, time after time, when everything pushed them to the ground. When the world is against you and the deck is rigged, that's the moment you choose your destiny. If you pick yourself up and stare down adversity, if you smile through missing teeth, if you spit out blood as you laugh in their face, it is then. That is when you are a true champion.

A champion is someone who goes to battle, looks into their opponent's eyes, and fights them with all the strength they have. A champion ignores the fear, ignores the pain. Nothing can stop them from getting up each time they fall down.

Even Rocky had the great line: *"It ain't about how hard you can hit. It's how hard you can get hit and keep moving forward. That's how winning is done."*

Every day we are faced with situations that require us to make decisions. Every choice we make is one step in a chain reaction. Each one leads to another. The important thing to realize through this process is that when once a choice is made, it has already become the past, and the one that follows becomes the present. You must understand that there's nothing you can do to change the decisions you have already made.

Often, we allow the past to influence the present. That, in turn, will impact our decision-making abilities. We become victims of our own mindset. In truth, we can control how we react and what we say. Our actions are always under our control. In fighting, it's easy for this to get in the way.

Here's a prime example: *The opponent I am supposed to be getting ready for is a killer on paper. He looks almost unbeatable. The fear of what he could do to me is already setting in. Sure, I'll train hard, but that doesn't change the danger he brings. How can I possibly beat him?*

The answer is surprisingly simple. He still needs to prove that when I am the one standing in front of him. If I let the fear over run me, I have already been defeated. But what could happen if I actually gave myself a chance? This is the mentality of how an underdog can shock the world.

Through my own hands-on experiences, I have learned that knowing and controlling yourself is the key to being a champion. As soon as we lose that control, the external forces take over, and Russian roulette begins.

When we fight for something, there are many battles that we go through before we reach the pinnacle of our journey. When we encounter the real fight, it is then that we face our emotions head-on—fear, anxiety, excitement, and so on. Just like in a video game, you have to win one level to progress to the next. When you reach the end, that's where the real enemy is lying in wait for you. That giant monster—with so many superpowers and all your tools has been depleted. After all, the last level is always the toughest. Some of us will get overwhelmed and give up upon reaching it, while some of us will stay determined and persevere, no matter how many times we fail.

But here's the thing—if someone else has ever achieved the impossible, that means the rest of us can too. Even that word is something to look at. Impossible. If you break it apart, it actually reads: *I AM POSSIBLE*. We just need to train ourselves to be ready for anything and everything that comes our way. In life, we must learn to accept and celebrate who we are and what we do. If you doubt yourself, how will you ever make anyone else believe in you?

Whether I have a good day or a bad one, I have to deal with it on my own. Some days are bright and breezy, some long and dark. If you learn to get through them all, you will succeed.

Do I weigh an extra few pounds? Am I heavier than I should be? Do I not meet beauty standards? Even if I am too heavy, it doesn't matter. Who sets those standards? Why do I even care about them? I love myself as I am, and I am comfortable in my skin; that's all that matters.

If you can truthfully respond in this way to these types of questions, you are on the right path. If you cannot, your battles are yet to be fought. Choose to be a champion. Control your thoughts, emotions, and actions. Be willing the face the monster that's standing across from you in the mirror.

 "I try to do the right thing at the right time. They may just be little things, but usually, they make the difference between winning and losing."

— KAREEM ABDUL-JABBAR

* * *

When I am in the locker room, All the fears come rushing in. I close my eyes, take a few deep breaths, and reset my mind. We walk down the tunnel; reset my mind. I enter the cage and reset my mind. The fight starts, and again I must reset my mind. Through each of these moments, I have to choose to not let fear dictate my fate.

Yes, I'm still terrified! But I don't have to give in to it. Being scared is no excuse for quitting. If you are looking for excuses, consider yourself a loser already. Nothing can get in the way of a real champion. I have trained myself for this. Once the battle begins, my choices need to become even quicker. I hit him, or he hits me. I need to recheck my mind and find the focus.

If I take too long to make a choice, I might never get a chance to do so again. My choice must be right, and the timing of it must be precise. I might start breathing heavily or feel tired, but none of that means I give in. I have to reset with every breath. I need to focus on the moment. Once the moment passes, I must move on to the next. No matter how hard the fight is, I have to force myself to keep going. These moments are all we ever truly have. It's a culmination of all the small achievements that will ultimately lead to an epic triumph.

"I hated every minute of training, but I said, 'Don't quit. Suffer now and live the rest of your life as a champion.'"

— MUHAMMAD ALI

* * *

Normal life is no different than that of a fight in the ring or cage. You need to make the right decisions. If you make a mistake, that's ok. Don't let it ruin the moment that follows. Take the hit and learn from it. We have to remind ourselves repeatedly that we are choosing to be a champion.

Shiny trophies, medals, fame, a seven-digit salary... sure, all that sounds nice. But those are not what define a Champion. They are merely the trappings of being a champion. The true winners in life are those who have a vision and those who see opportunities when others only see the impossible.

"Winning takes precedence over all. There's no gray area. No almosts."

— KOBE BRYANT

* * *

Being a champion does not require supernatural powers or really any exceptional features. Your attitude, effort, and persistence are all that matter throughout your fights. And that isn't limited to time in the ring. You can live like a champion in all walks of life, be it academics, relationships, sports, etc. With some hard work and perseverance, you can build a world for yourself where you are the only winner. The way you choose to live your life will define the outcome of all the tracks you set out on. If you surrender to the smallest of things in life, you will never stand tall when bigger battles are looming right in front of you.

What does that mean? It means I get out of bed, even when I don't want to. I get dressed, even on my lazy days. It means I take on new challenges that are going to push me beyond my comfort zone.

If we spend each day winning the little moments, the road ahead gets clearer, and the goals that seemed so far away become almost reachable.

Life is going to be life. It's going to knock us on our ass. But by cultivating an indomitable spirit, you will put yourself in a better position to rise above your downfalls and grant you the confidence and ability to get back up. You might be able to beat me, but I promise you this—you will never be able to defeat me. I am a champion because I choose to be a champion, and nothing can change that.

3

GROWING UP

> *"I allowed myself to be bullied because I was scared and didn't know how to defend myself. I was bullied until I prevented a new student from being bullied. By standing up for him, I learned to stand up for myself."*
>
> — JACKIE CHAN

* * *

Growing up, I always saw myself following in the footsteps of athletes I admired. My father was a big fan of the San Francisco Giants and 49ers. Ultimately, this made me one as well. I still remember standing in the bathtub, being no more than eight years old, listening to a baseball game on the radio.

My favorite player, Will Clark, was up to bat. The bases were loaded, and I played out a scenario where the ball was being thrown, and Clark smashed it out of the park for a grand slam on the first pitch. The pitcher wound up and fired the ball down the center of the plate.

CRACK!

The announcer yelled at the drive of the ball, and it was up and over the fence. He did it! My eight-year-old naked self-jumped up and down for joy in the bathtub, going completely nuts with happiness and excitement! I couldn't believe it. I felt like I'd manifested the exact scenario that'd just unfolded in real life. That was the unforgettable moment in which I established a connection between myself and that player. To this day, that experience remains a pivotal part of who I am. I started playing baseball as early as I can remember. I was probably just old enough to barely pick up a bat, put on a mitt, and make my best attempt to hit and throw the ball. I wanted to be just like my hero at the time, Will Clark. I went from being in a T-ball league in elementary school onward to junior high and then into high school. It was great. It was what I had always wanted. I felt it was my path to becoming a professional athlete. I even played first base, just like Will, and I was a lefty like he was.

However, there was one problem. I was...vertically challenged. In my freshman year of high school, I weighed just 98 pounds and was the shortest kid in my class. By the time I graduated high school, I wasn't even five feet tall! This ended up being a problem for me in a way that went beyond just becoming a baseball player. I was a prime target for bullies.

Throughout my childhood, I was bullied relentlessly and suffered physical and emotional abuse. Now, I know that we have all heard the saying that 'Kids can be mean,' and man, I learned that very early on. I still remember the first time that I got beat up, back in sixth grade.

One of the 'cool kids' liked to use me as his opportunity to make himself feel better. He did that through name-calling, shoving, or any other similar abuse you can think of from a twelve-year-old. If I saw him, I would usually hide to avoid bearing the brunt of the abuse that would be coming if he saw me. I remember telling my best friend (Levi) at the time that I was going to stand up to that kid and fight him, that it was something I needed to do on my own, and that he was not to jump in. That ended up being my first fight. It was also my first time facing the reality that I didn't know how to fight. Almost immediately after we started, he placed me in some type of chokehold that I simply couldn't escape. I can laugh about it now, given how ironic it is for me and how that would be virtually impossible today. When he let me go, I felt more defeated than I had ever been before.

The next year, I found myself being bullied yet again. And it was not just one person. But that meant I had another chance to redeem myself. I needed to stand up to another kid who had been picking on me all school year. If I didn't do it then it was never going to stop.

Of course, this followed the classic movie script of "Meet me at the playground after school tomorrow." I went to school the next day, mentally prepared to stand up to my bully AFTER class. But…things didn't exactly go as I had planned.

As soon as I arrived on campus, we saw each other standing at opposite ends of the hallway. Just as the morning's classes were starting, we both had that look of 'Well, here we are.' So, then and there, I dropped my backpack. He dropped his.

I still remember giving myself a quick pep talk, telling myself, "You have to hit him first."

I loaded my fist and began engaging forward. Then, something happened. Everything went black. I suddenly found myself on the cold, concrete floor. My head had smashed into the ground, causing me to lose all sight and feeling.

Once I was down, the bully and another person started pounding my face, my body, anything their hands and feet could reach. I felt paralyzed but could still hear the impact of their blows and the kids yelling at me, with reminders of why this was happening. The words, "Lay off, my homie," were repeated as if I were the one attacking them! There was nothing I could do to stop the beating until teachers finally pulled them off of me. My entire face was swollen, and I was bleeding from both of my eyes. To make matters even worse, the whole school watched it happen. Then came the icing on the cake—I was suspended from school for fighting.

Even though that wasn't my first lesson in adversity, it would become the catalyst for how most of my childhood would play out. After that fight, I was afraid to speak up. It was easier for me to just laugh it off when others made fun of me like it was all a funny joke. My self-confidence was nonexistent.

In life, we tend to block out things we don't want to remember. We set them aside, burying them deep in the recesses of our subconscious mind, hoping never to revisit them. After all, they are unpleasant memories that bring no joy in rehashing. When I was fighting for the WEC (World Extreme Cage Fighting, now the UFC), Yahoo! Sports did a story on me and bullying. I remember my mother calling me as soon as the article came out. I initially thought it would be one of those calls that went something like, "Great story, Chad! It was not. Instead, she spoke with intensity in her voice, asking me what the hell I was talking about. In the interview, they asked about my history and if I had been bullied while growing up. For whatever reason, I answered their questions as if I had just been a casual observer of bullying but had never experienced it personally. This was far from the truth. My mom felt it was an excellent time to remind me that I'd routinely come home from school crying.

My encounters with bullying were not exclusively relegated to the physical torment that most think of when they hear the word. My bullies came in the form of "friends." Their harassment was a daily occurrence, inflicted throughout my childhood. I was constantly made fun of for being the smallest guy in the group. I was called all sorts of names, like "short shit," "midget," kike," and every other offensive phrase you can think of.

And I didn't only have to worry about the bullies; there were numerous other problems. The city I lived in at the time was a breeding ground for gangs and financial turmoil within the community. My friends and I were constantly in trouble with either the law or other people. I needed to leave Sacramento. With the way things were going, I was heading in a dark direction. And fast. All the paths in front of me at the time were leading to either jail or, even worse, death.

Now, if the names and racism weren't enough, they were also accompanied by getting thrown into trash cans, held under bus seats, and picked on at parties, where my so-called 'friends' wanted to fight me so their egos would get inflated.

Like many abuse victims, I would go on to defend their actions by saying something like, "Oh, that is just so-and-so."

In my eyes, bullying was only something done by mean kids or gangs at school. I never really saw that it could be coming from within my circle of friends. My history of being bullied is what molded my childhood and my confidence (or lack thereof).

When certain words and phrases are repeatedly drilled into us, at a certain point, we come to believe them. We become programmed by them; we make them a part of our identity, like scar tissue. If someone keeps telling you that you are not good enough, you begin to believe that it's true. This has a higher likelihood of happening if you don't have the tools or strength to combat those words. Eventually, those words act as spells cast on us, and we start making them a part of our reality.

Humans are creatures of habit. When something gets repeated to us enough, we end up losing sight of the absolute truth. When a habit is influenced—and reinforced by pain—we begin to accept a life that is filled with pain. As time goes on, we become numb to what initially led us to that point. It wasn't until later on in life that I realized the habit of negative self-talk I'd developed was the bridge to precisely embodying what I had lacked all those years. It would lead me to have unstoppable self-confidence and an unwavering belief in myself. This is something I'm going to talk about later and in greater depth.

WRESTLING

I have always been an athlete. I started with baseball, followed by swimming, and then eventually wrestling. This was sort of a natural move for me to make since my dad had wrestled in high school. He was a state champion. When I started getting bullied in junior high, he thought that wrestling might help me. I had no idea what that was going to transform into so many years later.

As soon as I started wrestling in seventh grade, I fell in love with it. Yes, all sixty-seven pounds of me. There was just something about it. Maybe it was that it gave me the chance to fight back and defend myself when needed. Perhaps it was the challenge it offered me. I couldn't tell you exactly what it was, but there is one thing I can say for sure—I was hooked.

My passion for wrestling continued well into high school and eventually into junior college. Even as a high school freshman, I was still a mere 98 pounds. Despite that, I made the varsity team. To others, this would have probably been a massive confidence booster. Imagine that, the little guy making varsity! However, to me, I just saw it as, "Oh, no! These guys are bigger." As far back as I can remember, I would always find reasons for giving others more credit, more worthiness, and more of a right to be victorious than myself.

While in high school, I enjoyed a decent wrestling career. I spent four years on the varsity team, three of which were as team captain. I was also a three-time section qualifier, and during my senior year, I became a U.S. All-American by placing seventh at the National Championships. On paper, it all looks great, right? But there was a problem… I never believed that I could be a state or national champion. Sure, I worked hard and trained hard, and had natural athletic ability. Yet, I was still terrified of the competition.

I would go ahead and smash the opponents who would let me. I was a beast on the mat against the guys who were not at the top of the food chain. In almost clockwork-like fashion, my mind would find reasons to lose before a match against "ranked opponents" ever started. It could have been their credentials, their size, or even the simple fact they were in the finals of a major tournament. Whatever it was, without fail, I would create the outcome before it ever happened.

One of the most significant lines that I have ever read was a quote from Henry Ford, *"Whether you think you can, or you think you can't, you're right."*

I had always assumed that those wrestlers I was intimidated by had something extra. Something that I didn't. Remarkably, I never even questioned what that could be. In my mind, I was unable to see myself beating anyone who was top-ranked. Sure, I won a lot of tournaments and beat tough guys. However, every time I would face a legit competitor that I personally knew, I would allow the fear of who they were on paper to sabotage the match before we even stepped onto the mat.

Just before the end of my junior year, I again let my self-sabotaging ways dictate my path. I was at the section qualifiers, up against a kid who I'd beat earlier in the season. For whatever reason, I assumed he was not a challenge. That was a terrible mistake. He ended up beating me on points. This almost crushed any possibility of me making it to the state tournament. I still had two more matches, but my mind was already checked out. In a cloud of disappointment, I stormed off the mat and refused to talk to my coach. I couldn't help but think of myself as a failure. I wanted the day to end. As I left the gymnasium, there was a big steel door at the exit. Instead of opening it by the handle, I decided to punch it as hard as I could. How stupid could I be?!

The negative self-talk had won again. That time it had real consequences. My hand was shattered. I needed to find a way out of the tournament, and I did by doing that. Instead of quitting, I was able to use the excuse of my hand for pulling out.

The following year was my last chance. I finally made it to the state tournament and placed in the top four. This punched my ticket to Nationals and secured my spot in the biggest championship event of the country. I would now be up against the best wrestlers from every state. Another perfect opportunity for my insecurities to run wild! As I arrived at the arena, I looked over the tournament bracket so I had an idea of what the match-ups looked like. My first match was going to be against the Illinois state champion. Just as I'd expected, I was already starting to worry about my opponents' credentials. It's funny to me now, as I look back and see how the chronic cycles we fall prey to directly affect us so deeply when we're not even aware that we're in them.

That self-doubt had served as an odd kind of comfort zone for me. It was almost as if I had made the subconscious decision to lose the match. Like I'd completed some weird kind of calculus to validate how my opponent should win because their credentials were better than my own, making them more worthy of winning. As the match was playing out, it wasn't any different. I got wrecked. Wanna know the ironic thing? The other guy wasn't even better than me! I simply didn't perform. He hit the same throw on me 5x in a row. The final score was 10-4.

I was embarrassed. My last tournament in high school, and there I was, ending it with another sob story of "almost" or "could have." Shoulda, woulda, coulda. Lucky for me, it was a double-elimination event. I still had a chance. However, my coach was not on my side. Letting myself down was something I had gotten used to. This was different. I never realized that my actions could be letting down others as well.

"Let's just go home."

After my match, that was what Coach Bentley said to me. I didn't exactly understand at the time why he would say that. After all, the tournament wasn't over. He then followed up with, "There's no point for us being here. If you're just going to let these guys win, we might as well go home now and cut our losses."

Now, for me to place, I would almost need to do the impossible. I would have to win a match just to get back into the consultation brackets… then win all the remaining rounds until the semifinals. Of course, it wouldn't actually be impossible, but it would be very close to it. Based on my history, I would have a better shot at winning the lottery.

I convinced my coach to let me stay in the tournament. Something was different now. Previously, I had never felt that my actions were letting anyone else down. I'd always thought that it was just me doing it to myself and that others expected it. I knew that what was fast approaching was something that I had never done before. I would have to actually believe in myself to beat these guys.

Insert classical Rocky montage music

Round after round, I smashed my opponents. Two matches, three, then four. I was on fire. A victory in my next bout would guarantee a shot at being a U.S. All-American. I wanted to look at the brackets to see who the next match would be against. However, my coach knew what that would lead to and so didn't allow it. I'm incredibly grateful that he didn't. I was facing the three-time North Carolina champion. He had a ridiculous record of two-hundred-and-thirty wins, with just eleven losses. Not to mention, he had never been pinned. If I'd seen that, I know that my fears would have messed up everything for me. Instead, I continued down my path of destruction on the mat. I out-wrestled him fifteen to zero and then got the pin before the tech fall victory. I'd done it! I'd secured my spot to be in the top eight of the entire country.

I'd achieved what many people thought was an impossible feat—wrestled back into the tournament, overcame my doubts, and went on to beat some of the toughest wrestlers in the entire nation. That was the first time in my life that I had truly overcome adversity. Yet, the tournament was not over. I still had two more matches to go. If I won the next, I would continue and compete for third or fourth place. If I lost, I would be wrestling for seventh and eighth.

I was absolutely on fire, ready to battle any new monster that was put in front of me… or so I thought. My next match would be against another member of Team California. He was one of the top wrestlers in the state and had beaten guys that I had lost to.

"Here we go again," I said.

Who is the 'we' I was talking to? My limiting beliefs.

As soon as the match started, I was wrestling like shit. I think I ended up losing four to two or something close to that. However, the score didn't matter. My self-sabotage had taken over and prevented me from trying to win. Instead, I competed not to get finished. All I needed to do was not repeat my old habits, but I did. He went on to win third, and I pinned my next opponent in the finals for seventh place.

Although it was a significant achievement—becoming an All-American—it wasn't without the taste of bitter disappointment. I had fallen victim to myself yet again.

While writing this book, a young student of mine was going through almost the same situation during his high school wrestling section championships. His fear of letting people down and losing, along with extreme anxiety, had caused him to suffer a complete nervous breakdown. It'd all made him want to forfeit the entire event without even trying. I spent that morning attempting to calm him down on the phone, explaining that I knew exactly what he was going through. Hearing his raw emotions brought me directly back to those days, back when I was trembling in his shoes.

After going back and forth with him about finding strength and courage, he was still too locked in his doubts and ended up withdrawing from the event. I later found out that he did take part in one match. He won by pin and then removed himself from the rest of the event.

It amazes me how suffocating a fear of the unknown can be. We get locked into a state of doubt and allow ourselves to be immobilized by something that hasn't happened to us. What we end up doing is creating stories in our minds about why something won't work out. Sometimes, we even tell ourselves why other people are more deserving than we are. The resulting feelings of fear and thoughts of failing others are frightening, especially when we don't have the tools needed to overcome them.

After high school, I was scouted by several colleges for wrestling scholarships. Unfortunately, my grades were subpar. That meant attending a big school was out of the question. I'll admit that I was never the most remarkable student. There was even a two-year stint during high school competition season that I was forced to sit out due to my grades being too low. During my senior year, I was just happy enough to graduate and not get held back! Thankfully, one of the junior colleges—Sierra College—reached out to me with a great offer. The only stipulation was that I needed to maintain my grades at a decent level.

Once wrestling season got underway, I was excited. I wanted to make the necessary changes. But, of course, I fell back into my old habits. I started skipping classes, not doing my homework, and being utterly uninterested in the courses I was taking. In turn, my grades suffered. Then, in typical Chad fashion, I was unable to compete at the championship events due to my poor grades. After the second season of more of the same, I knew that it wasn't working out. I needed to start doing something different. It was time to make a significant change.

4

GETTING OUT

"Habits are formed by the repetition of particular acts. Feeling sorry for yourself and your present condition is not only a waste of energy but the worst habit you could possibly have."

— DALE CARNEGIE

* * *

S ince childhood, art has been my sanctuary. Creativity has always flowed through me. From getting in trouble for doodling all over my mom's work pads to sneaking out and spray painting around town, I have always found myself working on some kind of personal masterpiece. During high school, I managed to teach myself design software. I started doing commissioned freelance work and eventually won several art contests. Unfortunately, my junior college run was suffering because I was more concerned with partying and girls than academics. Something was becoming abundantly clear—my social environment needed to change.

Art school was my way out. I put together a portfolio and sent off applications. I had no idea what to expect, nor did I think anyone would actually respond. Favored by luck—and a tiny bit of decent work—two schools replied with acceptance letters. One was in San Francisco, and the other in Los Angeles. Having to choose between them was not a situation I was ready for. My first choice was San Francisco. The only issue was that it still neighbored Sacramento, only a ninety-minute drive away. I knew if I was that close to home, it would be all too easy for me to find reasons to travel back and slip into my bad habits. That decision was destined to change my life completely. The call had to be made, and the latter it was. "Los Angeles, here I come!"

Arriving in LA, I settled into the student housing unit I was assigned to share with three other guys. I was thrilled. It made me feel a sense of achievement that was unique and new to me. For the first time in my life, my actions were crossing the parameters of 'good performance' and even verging on 'amazing performance'. I made substantial industry connections and created a cartoon that showed promise and which flirted with getting picked up by major networks. *This is it!* I was doing so well, maintaining a near-perfect GPA while exploring the world of art. My projects were displayed all around campus. My parents were extremely supportive and proud of my decision. Everything was going as planned. Nothing was going to get in my way.

FACING A FEAR

We've all had certain things happen which have forever changed our path. Sometimes that's just trying something new. So, there I was, living the dream as an artist. Believe it or not, my journey into the world of professional fighting was an accident. Training MMA never crossed my mind. Who knew that a random fight in Tijuana, Mexico, would alter the course of my life and of what I was to become! Yet, here I am. When I first started fighting, I had no intention of pursuing it as a career. After all, MMA was only in its infancy. Not to mention, my weight class didn't even exist back then. There was also the whole issue of it not being legal in the state of California… or in most other states, for that matter.

Before I decided to pursue the life of an athlete, my goals were clear—graduate from art school, open my own studio and work on animated films. Maybe I'd even end up working for DreamWorks. I was hyper-focused on making these visions a reality. Everything I was building and developing was in service of making my dream a reality. There was just one problem…I was miserable.

I worked relentlessly on turning my dream into a reality. That meant everything from designing artwork for significant clients to partying with industry big wigs and celebrities. To most people, it would seem that I was already living the dream. However, that couldn't be further from the truth.

Ever since I was a kid, I have been an entrepreneur—from selling baseball cards out of my parents' garage to selling mistletoe from trees I'd climb (which I would end up falling out of and cracking my head open) to freelance artwork, which I started doing when I was 16-year-old. During my first year of art college, I met a like-minded artist—Michel Valenzuela—who had the same vision. Outwork everyone. We, together, later went on to do things that our school had never seen. We ended up opening our own studio that hired students and offered class credits and school instructors for work on major projects we had contracts for. This happened all while we were still enrolled. We re-defined the meaning of grinding every day. There was never too much work for us back then. To be honest, the more work we got, the more we would eat. We felt it was the life, as was the partying that came with it. Our studio became a popular hangout spot. We would work, then party, then work some more. At that point, I was smoking weed, daily packs of cigarettes, and doing cocaine, which eventually led to harder drugs like crystal meth.

After around two years of that, I began to hate everything I was doing. I hated working for clients. I hated going to school. But most of all, I hated what I was doing to myself. Another change was needed, and it had to be soon.

Being a wrestler, I figured that finding a good wrestling gym would blow away some of the bad habits I had developed. It would also help me get in shape and work toward becoming happy again.

I began searching for wrestling clubs, yet I couldn't find any gyms that offered it. Keep in mind; that this was 2004. MMA was still in its infancy, and Brazilian Jiu-Jitsu (BJJ) was not as popular as it is now. Having failed miserably in my quest, a friend offered to take me along to a Jiu-Jitsu class he was attending. I remember him saying that it was "like wrestling" and that I may like it.

My initial reaction was, "What the fuck is Jiu-Jitsu?"

Oh! The irony in that is hilarious to me now. I accepted his offer and gave it a try.

ENTER: THE ADDICTION

After my first class, I was completely hooked. Not only was I able to wrestle, but I was even allowed to choke people. *This is fantastic!* I couldn't believe that something like it even existed. It ended up helping me build a part of myself that had been missing for many years— the mastery of self-defense.

A few weeks into training, the class coach asked me if I would like to try out the MMA program they had during the evenings. And at the time, just like with Jiu Jitsu, I had no idea what MMA was. However, since I was enjoying the grappling class, there seemed no harm in trying it out. Once again, my mind was blown. Not only did I get to wrestle and choke people, but I was now even allowed to punch and kick them! A complete adrenaline rush. This was great. I started casually training somewhere between two and three times a week, so nothing serious. I remember one of the students reciting almost an encyclopedia's worth of names of guys that were fighting, yet I didn't recognize a single name he was talking about.

Somewhere around two months into it, the craziest thing happened. My coach asked me something that, once again, would end up changing my life forever.

"What do you think about doing a fight?"

Wait.

"A fight?" I replied in disbelief.

He laughed and said, "Yeah! I'm just throwing it out there. A show is looking for a lower-experience fighter to fight against a guy with around one year of training."

I remember being in a complete state of confusion. I hadn't even sparred! The only things we had done were some drills and minimal Jiu-Jitsu practice over the previous two months. Me... me actually FIGHTING was never even an option that I had considered.

So, out of curiosity, I asked, "Does it pay?"

He said, "Yeah, it's a pro-fight, so it pays. I don't know how much."

With that, the entire situation became surreal. I remember thinking that not only does this guy want me to fight, but he also wants me to participate in a professional fight (to his credit, there weren't any amateur organizations back then). The intrigue of the entire conversation had me deeply engaged.

I then asked, "When would it be?"

He chuckled to himself and told me, "Friday."

We had that conversation on the Monday before. Everything

that transpired over those next couple of minutes felt like a crazy dream. However, I asked anyway.

"Where is it?"

He chuckled again and said, "Tijuana, Mexico."

I just started laughing out loud. It all sounded like the script of some cheesy movie.

To give you some context as to why I thought it was so ridiculous, let's recap. At the time, I had only been training for two short months. I was still trying to kick bad habits, still hadn't sparred, and had failed every time I'd stepped up to face something that terrified me in the past. Then, suddenly, there was this man. This man who wanted me to go down across the border into Mexico and compete, for who knows how much money, in an actual professional MMA fight! To this day, I don't know how I managed to muster up the courage to squeeze out these five words, but I did.

"I'm down. Let's do it."

5

FIGHT IN MEXICO

"A brave man, a real fighter, is not measured by how many times he falls, but how many times he stands up."

— RICKSON GRACIE

* * *

Today, I am lucky that I can speak a little Spanish. But back then? Yeah, I could barely read off the Taco Bell menu. When I was offered the fight, we were told that all the hotel and accommodations would be taken care of beforehand. However, upon my arrival, I didn't need a translator to find out that I didn't have a hotel anywhere, and accommodations had most certainly not been arranged. I had to go through the hassle of traveling back across the border into San Diego to book a room. The beginning of the trip was already a hot mess. I couldn't believe what I was getting myself into. But one thing was clear; I wasn't being brought there to win.

As all Rocky stories go, this one went the same way. I would even make my entrance to The Eye of the Tiger soundtrack. Talk about fitting! While I was heading to the arena, I was unaware of what I should do or expect. Hell, I wasn't even a fan of fighting. I don't think I'd ever really even watched a fight before that day, let alone attended one.

Anyways, it was time to get wet. There is no better way to start swimming than to dive into the deep waters of the ocean, push your limits, and give your all to save yourself from drowning. We reached the venue, which was a three-story bar called The Baby Rock. That place was wild. Like, 90's action movie wild. It had the real feeling of an underground fight scene. You know, like one when someone always dies just before the hero has to face the bad guy. That place.

There were people all around. Some were there to watch the fight, and others just to party. The people who sat in the front row were expected to put their beers down and push the fighters back into the ring when they started falling out.

Backstage, my nervousness was killing me. I had no idea how to calm down. My anxiety was bubbling up and taking over. I began to stare at the wall in front of me and scream at it in an attempt to get myself into the mindset to fight. I was terrified and not sure what the hell I had gotten myself into.

 "When I don't know what I'm doing, I look like I don't know what I'm doing. When I'm excited or nervous, I look excited or nervous. And when I am lost, which is frequently, I look lost."

— **ELIZABETH GILBERT, EAT, PRAY, LOVE**

* * *

I thought I could play all my cards to prove my strength here. I even wore wrestling shoes, with the idea that they might intimidate my opponent by showing him that I was a wrestler!

My ears could hear something familiar, but my body was numb. Then the music started, which meant it was my time to face it. Time for me to appear in front of the crowd. We were the first fight of the night. The audience filled the hall with blood thirsty roars. I knew I was soon to face my entire childhood.

In true flashback fashion, I got beat up for three rounds. During each round, I came out swinging with street-style punches and kicks. Heading into the second round, my coach asked me to stop throwing my legs—because, let's be honest, I didn't know how to use them anyway—and I might have saved myself a lot of embarrassment if I'd taken his advice. However, I was too stubborn and didn't listen.

Sometimes you understand things as they are. You may also agree with the advice you keep receiving from people around you. Yet, the subconscious mind can still make you act in a very different way, and I guess that is exactly what was happening to me. I was unable to process anything that made sense, acting only on dumb impulses.

I immediately charged my opponent and threw another kick. He successfully blocked it and suplexed me down on my head. After the slam, he took my back and almost choked me out. I could feel death sitting right beside me, looking me straight in the eye. I knew if I gave up at that moment, I would continue to give up at every hurdle. Somehow, I kept pushing forward.

I managed to escape and ended up in the top position. I was exhausted. When the round ended, the referee even had to help pick me up off the canvas to guide me back into the corner.

As the third round started, my energy was gone. That made it very easy for my opponent to take me down. When I hit the canvas, I gasped for air and could barely breathe. With one minute left in the fight, I managed to reverse the position. I ended up on top and saw his neck. I grabbed it and squeezed it with everything I had. HE TAPPED OUT!

I did it. Somehow, I'd secured a choke that made him quit using a guillotine that I'd learned just a week before the fight. It wasn't just the victory that overwhelmed me, but also the white envelope filled with $150 cash. That was my first adult taste of YES! I CAN.

UNPLUGGING FROM THE MATRIX

One of the most common questions I get asked is, "What is it like to fight?"

Over the years, my answer to that question has continuously evolved. I'd like to say otherwise, but in truth, I have given all the expected cliché responses like, "It's the most incredible feeling!" and "It's a pure adrenaline rush!" and so on.

These days I've got a much better answer. It's one that is pretty simple to explain. Fighting is a pure moment, one in which you are completely unplugged from the Matrix we live in every day. That includes the stresses of everyday life—paying bills, working, dealing with family, etc.—because once the fight begins, none of those distractions matter. But more than that, during a fight, it's like they don't exist. The only thing that does is the danger staring you right in the face.

Life tends to throw things at us that will make us blind to our goals. We quickly forget our WHY. When you are fighting, the only thing that matters is staying in the present moment. We zone in and become hyper-focused on the challenge directly in front of us. For five seconds or fifteen minutes, we stay entirely unplugged and free from everything we have to deal with in our everyday lives.

After my first fight, something inside me changed. I couldn't quite figure out what it was, at least not at that time. However, what I felt was something special. I had finally faced a significant fear, conquered it, and won. In doing so, I made my decision to take the red pill and dive deep into the rabbit hole. And just like taking the red pill was for Neo, there would be no going back for me.

6

YOUR TRUTH COMES OUT WHEN IT'S NOT FUN ANYMORE

"You gain strength, courage, and confidence by every experience in which you really stop to look fear in the face. You are able to say to yourself, 'I have lived through this horror. I can take the next thing that comes along.' You must do the thing you think you cannot do."

— **ELEANOR ROOSEVELT**

* * *

Over the years, I have watched and coached countless fights. I have seen people excel under pressure. But I have seen even more people break under the weight of it. This remains true even among athletes of the highest-level. I have watched world champions break down into tears due to fear and anxiety before a fight. I was no different.

After my fight in Mexico, I went back to working full-time. But it wasn't the same. My mind would drift to thoughts about wanting to train.

Over the next year, I began watching DVDs, did a few Jiu-Jitsu tournaments, and found myself at the gym more and more. I was getting obsessed with the sport. Then it finally happened. MMA was becoming legal in the state of California.

As news broke, a startup promotion called the Total Fighting Alliance (TFA) contacted me and asked if I wanted to fight in the very first sanctioned California event. I jumped on the historic opportunity.

The show matched me up with a guy from Brazil. Now, we need to remember that this was before the likes of YouTube and social media. Back then, I could not research who I was going to be fighting. I knew that if someone was from Brazil, they surely had to be a Jiu-Jitsu wizard… or related to the Gracie family.

Of course, this made my mind spin. Anxiety began eating me alive. Thoughts tumbled and rushed through my head about what kind of killing machine this guy must be. I needed to find a mental off-switch to flip so I could silence my insecurities and have my opponent see me as a threat. I needed to become my own superhero.

I think everyone, even fighters themselves, can agree that the idea of fighting is scary. There is a significant fear of the unknown, as well as the fear of failure. These are natural feelings that can cripple you in any situation. However, if we find a way to harness them, these same feelings can serve as fuel to propel us to new heights of greatness.

As the date of the fight drew closer, I knew that regular old Chad was not going to be the one who beats this guy. I didn't have enough confidence in myself. I needed something more. I needed an alter ego. That's when I decided to shave my head, leaving just a mohawk. I could play the role of some unhinged, "crazy" fighter.

At weigh-ins, I looked the part of a tough guy. Chests were flared out, and dirty looks were exchanged as we stood in front of each other. As terrified as I was, I didn't want to show it. I couldn't. He needed to see how crazy I was. It's funny now when I look back at it. Today, I see similar acting 'tough guys' as a joke. I can see right through their silly bravado. It's all a show. But that's what I needed at the time. I needed a distraction, and a show is a great one. So, I put one on in the form of a fake persona to hide the fear of how I really felt.

As soon as the fight started, I began pacing back and forth in the cage, waiting for the bell to ring while hitting myself in the head. When it rang, I somehow found the fear and channeled it into the character I'd developed. They molded together into one. I was fighting at a high pace, throwing my opponent all over the cage. In one exchange, I pushed him against the wall, flipped him upside down, and slammed him to the canvas from over my head.

In the second round, I stepped in with a left hand that dropped my opponent to the floor and covered the canvas with blood. This punch eventually led to the doctors stopping the fight and me winning by technical knockout. That was how I won my second professional MMA bout and created an alter ego that would later become my superhero.

After that fight, my desire for competition and training was peaking. We had MMA launching legally in California, and there I was, with two wins and no losses. The next show was only four months later, so I jumped on it as fast as I could. Another opportunity for my alter ego to overshadow my fears. However, I wanted to exceed my appearance from the last fight. I decided to still go with the mohawk look again but dyed it multicolored. I even had a rap artist walk me down the tunnel into the cage, where the sold-out crowd was already roaring with hungry fans. MMA was on the verge of blowing up.

As my music started, I entered the arena. The crowd went crazy. The show was an absolute hit. I stepped into the cage and continued doing my signature back-and-forth pacing. The fight started, and I charged my opponent. He took me down, but I secured an arm lock that nearly finished the fight. We briefly exchanged strikes, I threw my first-ever head kick that barely missed, and he went for another takedown on me. This time I grabbed his neck, rolled him to his back, and squeezed for my life. He tapped.

I'd done it! I'd won again. I let go of my opponent's neck and screamed a la Chuck Liddell, spreading out my arms in a primal victory celebration. I now had three wins as a fighter, and my alter ego was the driving force of what would soon turn into my career. The high of finishing an opponent is almost indescribable. I think many fighters will agree. Once the bout is called off, there is a rush of adrenaline that explodes throughout your body. And in the moments that follow, it can almost seem like temporary insanity. We scream, we cry, and we jump on the cage. Raw emotions overcome us. It's intoxicating like a drug. A high that only in that moment you can ever feel.

After that fight was when promoters started to market me. I began doing press interviews and was a part of media days for the show. That eventually led to them offering me an opportunity to fight for the Bantamweight Championship title— yet another first for the state of California. It would also become my first loss as a professional.

Leading up to my first title fight, I trained my ass off... at least, at the time, I thought that was what training my ass off meant. I sparred, I grappled, and I did conditioning. I even signed up at a real boxing gym. Back in those days, boxers wanted nothing to do with MMA guys. They saw us as wild, crazy people. Not real fighters. When I would come into the gym, the other coaches and even the gym owner paid me no attention. I was the like the loner kid, the crazy one who played by himself. I had to hire guys to teach me privately. Even then, I still wasn't given much of a shot.

They tried to push me out in any way possible. I remember the first sparring session I did with one of the more prominent boxers. We touched gloves, and everyone in the gym knew he was going to put them on me. I cracked him with a left hand on the chin. It dropped him to the canvas. The entire gym gasped. He picked himself up, and I gulped at the realization that I was going to pay dearly for that. He started bouncing around with much more intensity than before. Then it happened. He hit me in the head, and that opened up a devastating shot to my liver. That was the first time I had ever been hit in the body. I dropped to the floor and rolled around, gasping for air. It was the worst pain I had ever been in. The coach waived off the session and sure expected me not to come back. But I did. Day after day, I showed up and just wouldn't go away. Eventually, he began holding up his fingers when I got there to signal how many rounds of jump rope I needed to do. Sometimes it was three rounds, other times non-stop for an hour. I didn't care because I loved the work and wasn't going to stop. It was soon after that when they started to hold pads for me and even began coaching my sparring sessions. Slowly, I was becoming 'their MMA fighter.'

Soon there were only a few days left before the big day. I had to build up the courage and confidence to show up. Even though I was undefeated, I would be stepping up to face a real fighter. He was someone who I pictured must be a monster who was fighting for a championship title. Again, this is exactly what I did when I was younger with wrestling. And that sure as hell never went my way!

As the fight began, I entered the cage with my musical performer and the persona I had created. Once the bell rang, terrified, I charged straight at my opponent. We exchanged a few strikes, and then the action broke momentarily. I took a deep breath, faked a kick, and followed it with a heavy left hand that dropped him to the floor. The crowd went insane. He was almost entirely unconscious. In a blind state, I followed him to the canvas and tried to unleash a flurry of punches. One of the shots seemed to wake my opponent up. This allowed him to recover and then do the unthinkable. During my reckless attack, he reversed the position, took my back, and choked me. I lost. I was on the edge of victory and broke mentally when he made it competitive.

After the fight, I wanted to quit and go back to work. Failure was something that my childhood had gotten used to. It would be the easy way out. I could have made a million excuses—and honestly, I probably did—but something inside me didn't let that happen. A few weeks passed, and the promotion offered me a rematch. They said the fight was so exciting that they wanted to see it again. It was another chance for me to stand up, face adversity, and not back down.

Training for that fight would require me to get out of my comfort zone. I needed to get focused and train like a professional... even though I didn't know what that looked like. Most of the MMA training I had done was only with a few hobbyists, tucked in the back of a Taekwondo school. It was time for a much-needed change of atmosphere.

I had received an invite to train in Northern California with Former UFC Middleweight Title Contender Dave Terrel. At the time, Dave was a big name in the sport. It would be my first-time training away. I was to receive royal treatment, complete with luxurious room and board… so there we were, me and two other guys, staying in the attic space of his gym. A small fridge, a microwave, and sleeping bags. Five. Star. Luxury.

Every day we woke up to the ringing bells and yelling of the 6 A.M. morning classes. We would crawl out of the tiny space and usually go for a morning run, then eat breakfast and train at noon (sometimes, I would even take the morning class). This was followed by either a technical striking class or Jiu-Jitsu in the evening. Every day I was exhausted, but there was something special about not having any other obligations. I would wake up, train, and sleep in the gym. For three weeks, my life was solely dedicated to one thing. Laser-focused. It was also the first time I had ever seen someone get put to sleep by a choke in training.

It happened on sparring day. I don't remember who did it, but I remember what happened. One of the guys who shared the attic with me was caught in a rear-naked choke and refused to tap during a roll. This made his body go limp, and he started snoring. Dave walked over and stood directly over him, waiting for him to begin to wake up.

As he did, Dave yelled, "Why are you in my room???!!!!"

The kid kicked and screamed in fear. That was one of the funniest things I had ever seen. The whole room broke out into laughter.

After our sparring days, we typically went for a big run. That camp showed me what I needed to do if I wanted to take MMA seriously. Once my training in Northern California ended, it was time to fight my fears again.

The sold-out crowd in Santa Monica Civic Center chanted, "SAVAGE!" throughout the auditorium.

I was ready to face my fear. The fight started, and once again, my opponent took me down. Only this time, it was me who reversed the position and took his back. I locked in the rear naked choke, and it was over.

It was that fight that showed me what sacrifice and focus could do. I'd achieved something that I would never have imagined myself capable of. It was time to take it to the next level.

7

DROPPING OUT OF SCHOOL & MOVING INTO MY CAR

 "The most important thing is this: To be able at any moment to sacrifice what you are for what you will become."

— ERIC THOMAS

* * *

We've become accustomed to hearing the impossible stories of others who struggle and sacrifice while battling obstacles in pursuit of success. Rejection and failure are universal. At some point, everyone tastes the bitterness of adversity. Even Michel Jordan—arguably the greatest basketball player of all time—didn't make the varsity line-up.

When seeing others accomplish the unthinkable, people tend to say things like, "Man, I don't know how they could do that!"

But here's the thing... when you find something that drives you to the point of obsession, you get a glimpse of why and how others were able to get to the level they did.

During my career, I have had to make countless hard decisions. One of the hardest was when I chose to leave school, leave my job as an artist, and move into my car to pursue this fighting thing that came with next to zero chance of earning a living.

Usually, when I tell this part of my story and talk about me being homeless, the initial reaction from people is, "Oh shit." But it was a choice. I put myself there. And like I said, when I was going to school, on the surface, at least, everything looked incredible. My grades were good; I was working full time, owned my studio, and was twelve units away from graduating with my bachelor's degree. Why the hell would I leave that?! Good question. Looking back, the answer was simple. I was miserable. Fighting and training had given me so much more than doing artwork for clients ever did. It allowed me to start learning about myself. To finally begin facing all the demons that were lurking from my past. For the first time in my life, I had found something that gave me a chance to become more powerful than all my fears.

After winning my first championship, fighting was all that I could think of. In the art studio, I would playfully punch and kick my collogues. In stores and markets, I would shadow-box invisible opponents like a crazy person. I was obsessed. This was where my nickname, "The Savage," originated. I couldn't sit still.

One day in the studio, I kept hitting one of the artists, and he said, "Savage, stop beating everyone up every day. Save it for the ring." I remember laughing about it, but then everyone started joking around and calling me Savage instead of my actual name. My alter ego was manifesting. He could not be contained.

My days at the gym started getting longer, and those spent at my art studio got shorter. I would find any reason to get more training. This, of course, did not sit well with my partner at the studio. I needed to make an actual decision. Do I commit to the art industry? I had already spent almost a hundred thousand dollars on student loans to pursue that dream…or do I risk everything by trying to make this fighting career a thing, with next to zero chance of making a living from it?

Looking back, it was a crazy decision. I knew that if I did go all-in on fighting and it didn't work, I could always go back to art. I had my portfolio, and I could even go back to school and finish the remaining credits I needed for the bachelor's degree. So, I did it. I dropped everything. I had next to no savings. I gave my entire studio and all of its equipment to my partner.

I said, "Fuck it. I'm doing this."

It was terrifying. I would have to fight to make a living and shave down my expenses to the absolute minimum. That meant moving into my car—a beat-up 1992 Toyota Celica. In my mind, my plan was utterly foolproof. It just had to succeed. If you sacrifice everything, there's no way you can fail. Boy, was I wrong.

Over the next fourteen months, my entire life became about fighting in one way or another. I had seven fights across the country, along with one in Canada. Three of those were for a big event at the time called Bodog Fight. It was my first experience fighting for a top promotion and on TV. Names like Jorge Masvidal, Gegard Mousasi, Yves Edwards, and even Fedor Emelianenko were just a few of the pioneers who were fighting for them.

My first fight was in Vancouver, Canada, and it was a much better experience than when I fought in Mexico. The show picked us up from the airport in a limo. It took us around the town and even had an entire training facility built into the hotel for us. It was incredible. I wish I could say the fight went as well as the experience.

The day before weigh-in, the promotion changed the opponent on me. They said it was a better match-up for me.

What they should have said was, "good luck." Bodog didn't have my weight class—one hundred and thirty-five pounds—but my original opponent was about the same size as me and had roughly the same experience. It made sense for me to make this big of a jump in the promotion. But my new opponent? He was a much larger and more experienced fighter from Sweden.

All my insecurities came crashing in like a freight train once we hit the floor. I took him down. He reversed the position, and all I could think about was how big he was. This would lead to me yet again losing by rear-naked choke.

In the next few fights, I found some success, along with more losses. My career wasn't seeming like it was going to turn into anything special. I had built a very unimpressive record of five and four, though I had won some fights and been in some great events. But to call it a profession at that time, well, I couldn't do that. I think the most significant payday I had at the time might have been $2,000.

Sure, for a guy living out of his car, that's ok. But to say it made sense to leave my career in pursuit of that... I don't think so. Something had to change, and it did. Things were about to get worse.

THE UGLY COUSIN OF FIGHTING

There's an ugly cousin that comes with fighting, and it's not the injuries. It's the unspoken reality of all skin infections. Especially when you're broke, have no insurance, and are living in your stinky-ass car.

Our gym eventually moved out of the Taekwondo school we had started at and into a big corporate gym at the time called 'Bodies in Motion.' This gym gave us our own private mat area, punching bags, and even a boxing ring.

Through years of wrestling, I'd had my share of ringworm. When you're in close contact with so many people, all dripping sweat, it's bound to happen. Mix that in with a big corporate gym and thousands of people walking on the mats with outside shoes, and you get a cesspool waiting to grow. I found that out the hard way. I'd wrestle on those mats and have no care in the world until I had a big itch on my face. One day I thought I had been scratched, and maybe it had gotten infected. Sadly, I was mistaken. I ended up getting a massive case of ringworm that stretched across my face and neck. It was *huge*. Everyone could see it. After about a week of putting tons of fungal cream on it, the infection subsided and finally went away. Now, you would think I had learned my lesson. Don't put your face where people walk. It's common sense, right? But I guess common sense isn't so common. At least, not with me.

About six months later, I would come to learn about something much worse than ringworm. I was deep into training for my next fight when I noticed a bite mark on my arm. It hurt like hell. Over the next few days, the pain got worse, and my arm swelled to the point that it was no longer bearable. The only way I could handle it was by resting it above my head. Training was not even possible. Despite being stubborn and without insurance, I finally went to the doctor to get it looked at. After the exam, they took a culture sample and believed I had been bitten by a brown recluse spider, but would not know for sure until the results came back.

Within twenty-four hours, the clinic called me and said I needed to see them ASAP. That's not something you ever want to hear from a doctor. I rushed down to the facility, and they told me I had not been bitten by a spider but had a severe MRSA bacterial staph infection in my arm that had begun rapidly spreading. They even said that if the infection continued to spread into my armpit, I might have to lose my arm to stop it from getting into the lymph nodes and spreading through my entire body.

Once admitted to the hospital, they cut the wound open and

began draining the infection. It was something that I can only describe as a horror movie. They squeezed a green sponge-like ooze from my arm that seeped out like a tube of toothpaste. Though the infection started midway down my forearm, it had quickly spread to the middle of my bicep and was roughly three inches away from the lymph nodes in my armpit. I was lucky. The pain was almost instantly gone, and all that was left was a quarter-size hole that was stuffed with gauze. Great. Except I then needed to figure out how to pay the hospital bill.

After that big scare, I realized I needed to have insurance. I didn't have the money for it, and my financial problems became increasingly real day by day. The temptation of quitting and going back to art seemed like an easy way out, but I wanted to keep going. I needed to find a way to make more from fighting. Asking for financial help from friends was at the end of its course, and, to be honest, it was getting to be a bit embarrassing.

THE BEGINNING OF TEACHING

One of my buddies had been teaching group fitness classes at the gym. He offered to recommend me if I was interested in becoming an instructor… though I had no idea how to teach. I barely knew how to throw a punch. Luckily, these were not technical classes. You just had to tolerate loud music, yell at people through a headset microphone, and make them sweat. I did a trial class and got the job—my first fitness gig. Looking back, I can't believe it was how I started. I guess we all start somewhere. I think Dana White—the president of the UFC— started out doing the same thing.

As funny as those days were, the characters I would meet along the way would become endless. This one class stands out in my mind when a guy was trying to murder the punching bag.

As I interrupted his fierce battle and tried to correct his form, he stopped, looked at me, and said, "I DON'T CARE!"

I shook my head and walked off. Then I saw him continue to hit the bag like an angry, wild, inflatable balloon man. It was hard to watch. But over the years, I've seen those guys everywhere I look. You probably have, too. Hopefully, you are not one of them. After teaching classes for a while, I made enough money to eat, put gas in my car, and pay for training up to my next fight. I loved it. Things went from a single class to teaching several a week. I started to get the hang of the whole teaching concept. However, I still needed a better lifestyle. Living out of my car was getting old.

After giving it much thought, I decided that maybe it was time for me to start offering private lessons. I would see other instructors with individual clients lined up throughout the day. I remember thinking, *Hey, that looks way easier than a big group class. I can do that, no problem.* Well, there was a problem. I didn't have any certifications... and in most fitness environments, that is a must, and it's next to impossible to teach without them.

LIFE AS A 'PROFESSIONAL'

Fighting is an interesting 'professional' sport. There are no certifications, degrees, or even standards as to what it even means... well, outside of the whole "I get punched in the face for money" thing! Sure, I did pay a fee to the state that allowed me to fight. But that's it. After doing that, anyone could potentially say they were a professional fighter. You could be 0-10 and still be considered a pro on paper!

When I first asked about teaching private lessons, the coordinator of the fitness gym asked me, "What certifications do you have?"

I didn't have any and knew full well that I was trying to bullshit my way into the position.

The only response I could give was, "You can watch my

fights online. Being a professional fighter is the only credential I have."

It worked. I was in a gray area the gym didn't have a response to. In their eyes, I must have known what I was doing since I was a professional. I laugh about it now because oddly— and kinda unbelievably—the gym ran with it! They used the opportunity to say there was a professional fighter available for group classes and private lessons! I mean, why not? They took 80% of what the client paid and gave me the remaining 20. It was a massive win for them. Kind of a rip-off for me, but I didn't care. I used it as an opportunity to learn how to teach, market myself, and begin building a solid fan base.

My schedule quickly became packed with clients, and I became a star attraction at the gym. Members would gather to watch me train, and my classes were slammed. It was a home run for everyone. After a while, I started making decent money. I guess I was putting my skills to better use, and it was then that I finally began seeing how I could make a living from fighting. While making money wasn't even the best part, it did allow me to finally get out of my car and move into a small studio apartment. It was great. Things finally started taking a turn in the right direction.

Over the years, I have coached countless students and hundreds of individual clients. One of those individuals who came into my life would go on to become someone that was not only a friend and mentor on many levels but also someone who'd plant the seed of an idea that would grow to change my life.

8

FIGHTING BECAME A WAY OF LIFE

 "It's not the will to win that matters – everyone has that. It's the will to prepare to win that matters."

— BEAR BRYANT

* * *

FORESHADOWING (SIDE STORY)

Foreshadowing is really just another name for Déjà vu. Sure, perhaps you've experienced it in some small way, but it's something that usually only happens significantly in movies. You know what I'm talking about... the hero has a vision of some future event, and the whole scenario plays out before it happens. Real life doesn't generally work like that.

It was years before I fought in the WEC when I first met Jon Putnam. He would go on to become a longtime friend and mentor. Back then, he was the owner of a clothing manufacturer which produced accessories for another company. Although unknown at the time, that outfit—called *Tapout*—would go on to explode into the largest apparel brand in the sport.

Jon was working with a few fighters for the UFC and the WEC (the UFC was the premier league for one hundred-and-fifty-five-pound weight classes and above, while the WEC focused on the lighter weights, down to one hundred and thirty-five pounds). One day, he invited me to join him at a WEC event in Las Vegas. He wanted me to see what the best fighters in the world looked like in person and experience the excitement of the BIG show. We jumped on a plane. Then there we were, at the *Hard Rock Casino*. It was the first time I'd seen what the pinnacle of the sport looked like in person. Until then, I could never have pictured myself on that stage. It had always seemed so far away, so alien. But being there that day gave me a sense of belonging.

It was as if the spark of passion I'd always carried was finally set ablaze. Like gasoline was poured on top. And the flames rushed through me, and I remember telling Jon, "I'm going to fight here one day." He smiled, then told me that was precisely why he'd wanted me to come with him. I will forever be grateful to him for that day, for opening my eyes to the endless possibilities of where fighting could take me. It was the dawn of a much bigger vision.

THE TRANSITION

The way we train today is vastly different from when I first started building my team. Every day was war. There was no real direction for how to prepare. Nobody I knew personally had turned it into a full career, not yet, and the trainers were only coaching as a hobby. Back then, to get ready for a fight, we did one thing. We fought. Every day, we fought.

As I started gaining more experience and building connections with other athletes, I began reaching out to guys to help me train. It started with some of the locals. One friend would invite their friend, and before long, we had a solid group of up-and-coming fighters. Word soon got out about our training. Eventually, guys who were actually in the UFC started coming in as well; Mac Danzig, Dan Hardy, Andy Wang, Gabe Ruediger, and even heavyweight champion Josh Barnett. These became not only the guys I looked up to but also my daily training partners. There was always a crackling intensity in the room. It was inspiring. I tried to learn as much as possible, even when that meant them punching my head in… which happened much more often than not!

We would typically run two to three miles before practice, spar hard, eat some food, then rinse and repeat the process at night. If my body wasn't too badly beaten up, I would even add a third session somewhere in the day. It was *brutal*. If I'm honest, I was afraid of every session. I just didn't want them to know it. I had to fake it and act like I belonged in the room.

Twice a week, on sparring days, I would do ten rounds of boxing. Every round meant a new partner would rotate in on me —known as "Shark Tanking"—and I remember being knocked out in exchange one time after being hit on the chin with a hook. My body folded. I fell into the ropes backward. From what I was told, I bounced off and kept swinging. One of my teammates had to interrupt the session and force me to get out of the ring.

Shortly after, our team began growing. We had an opportunity to leave the corporate gym and bring our training to a new facility that was going to be designed for MMA. That move would also mark the beginning of my education in learning how to run a gym.

I treated the place like it was mine; creating all the programs, teaching the classes, and doing all the marketing. I even launched my own clothing brand. It was the perfect opportunity I'd been waiting for to blend my artistic background and fighting. It was like a jigsaw puzzle had finally started clicking into place.

FIGHTING

Up until then, my parents had no idea what I was doing. I'm not sure what they would be more upset by; the fact I'd left my career or that I'd dropped out of school. Either way, it wasn't going to be a good conversation!

But that changed when I finally got a big win that would define and ignite my career. It was my last fight with Bodog and also the first time I would fight in Vegas.

I remember giving some crazy prediction to a reporter, "It's going to be a wild finish. Who knows, maybe even a dragon will come down from the sky."

I had no idea what the hell I meant when I said that. But it sure set the tone.

The fight started and I was a man possessed. Thirty-seven seconds in, and it was over. A colossal takedown, slam, and relentless strikes. I don't know if I manifested it from the interview, but I sure delivered what I'd foretold—a wild finish. The feeling was indescribable. I could feel the roar of the crowd in my bones, and I knew that this would be the start of a new me.

My next fight was for a second championship title. I figured it was finally time to tell my parents and invite them to come to see me. They'd always supported me during wrestling, but this was different. They had no idea what MMA even was.

I remember the first conversation with my dad.

"Hey, I want you to come and watch me fight."

His response was golden. "Fight what?"

I guess I didn't know what I expected him to say, but it wasn't that. To my surprise, they were actually really supportive.

The fight came, and I won by third-round TKO. It was one of the most monumental moments of my career. My dad became my number one fan. He liked to play fantasy manager and tell me who I should be fighting. It was amusing at first, but over time it began to feel as if nothing I did was ever good enough. My victories were always overshadowed by a remark from him that seemed to detract from the moment. It wasn't until years later that he eventually gave me credit for what I was doing.

Over the next year, my mindset began to shift. I started believing I could actually beat these guys. Training became an obsession. I was constantly looking for new ways to elevate myself. This even led to the hiring of a breathing coach. We started with basic yoga, meditation followed, and then swimming became an almost daily routine. Soon after, the exercises all became one. I started doing lung development underwater by running focused mental drills that forced me to sink to the bottom of a pool. Some days I would hold a brick and walk laps as far as I could. Others were spent on timed exercises to simply see how long I could hold my breath. In the beginning, I was terrible. But as the weeks went on, I was able to get my numbers up to three and a half minutes on a single breath.

The training was paying off. I built up a five-fight winning streak. I won another title in Oklahoma, growing my record to nine to four. I even took a trip to Japan and trained with MMA legend Rumina Sato, who would later become a good friend. The timing was everything. My next fight would be one of the toughest of my career and one that forced me to understand what being a champion really meant.

 "Winning takes you to hell."

— TIM GROVER

* * *

I had started working on my striking full-time with a new boxing coach, Seb Zewdie. Seb was an Olympian for Ethiopia and also the Olympic trials coach for Trinidad and Tobago. We had worked together a bit before the fight, but I put him in the driver's seat that time. He pushed me to heights I didn't know I could reach. We would run a 10k on the track weekly. I had targeted punch count goals. We worked daily on my reflexes and footwork. I began sparring with top contender boxers. With every passing day, I was finely tuning the beast within me.

When the day of the fight arrived, I was sick of training. I wanted a real fight. And that's exactly what I got, from bell to bell. Fifteen minutes of epic madness—a complete war. For the first time in my career, I experienced how two fighters are completely locked in the zone. I was forced to rely on my unwavering determination and dig down deep to see how badly I wanted to win.

My face was split open to the bone during the first round by an elbow that covered my entire head in blood. Back and forth, we both attacked and came close to submissions. The second round was more of the same, almost finishing each other on multiple occasions. The audience cheered on the fury. In the third round, I shot in as he threw a body kick at the same time. It sounded like the crack of a bat as his shin smashed into my face. I finished the takedown but was knocked out. I woke up in his guard but somehow managed to keep fighting. The final bell would ring as I was on his back, attempting to finish a rear-naked choke. It was going to the judges. I had no idea how they were scoring it. My mind was still busy processing the bloody fight that we'd just had. Then it was announced—a split decision. The first judge called it for me. The second for him. It was all resting on the final scorecard.

I closed my eyes and heard the announcer, "Judge three scores the fight twenty-nine and twenty-eight for your winner, by split decision," then a long pause that felt like hours crawling by.

"Chad George!" I screamed.

Tears of joy rolled down my bloody face. A current ran through my body as the adrenaline wore off. I'd earned that feeling. Most people will never understand—let alone experience—what it feels like to have poured everything you have into something like that. How I felt at that moment was not just about winning the fight. I could finally see that all my sacrifices had paid off. That was when I realized I was a fighter. Other people noticed as well.

9

A DREAM TO A NIGHTMARE

"Everybody said: 'Follow your heart' I did. It got broken."

— HERECULE POIROT

E very athlete dreams about competing in the big leagues. Football has the NFL, basketball has the NBA, and baseball has MLB. For MMA, it's the UFC (Ultimate Fighting Championship). Back when I was just starting out, the UFC didn't even have my weight class. Despite fighting really being a passion for us little guys, we had no big league to legitimize it until the WEC came along. The demand for small fighters was rising. The UFC's parent company, *Zuffa*, decided to purchase an event called World Extreme Cage fighting (WEC). They wanted to turn it into a show the UFC would hold for lower-weight classes (below one-hundred fifty-five pounds). Every fight was action-packed, and each card was exhilarating from top to bottom. As the signings to the show started to increase, my name began circulating as a top prospect. It soon became clear I needed to get signed… since I was ten to four as a professional and on a six-fight win streak, it was only a matter of time until it happened.

And suddenly, it did. After the war in my last fight, The WEC called and offered me a contract if I was willing to step up on a two-week notice. *Holy shit!* I accepted the fight and signed. I was going to have my promotional debut and be on a roster with the best fighters in the world. *Las Vegas, here I come... AGAIN!*

When I signed with the WEC (now the UFC), I thought I had made it. It was the big leagues. It was what I had worked so hard for. It was what I had sacrificed and struggled for. I'd be on the stage with the best fighters in the world. A dream I'd manifested. There was only one problem. It meant I'd have to FIGHT against the best fighters in the world. Like many other things, the idea of it once again terrified me. Luckily, before my first fight, I really didn't have much time to think. The promotion offered me a guy I had never heard of, John Hoseman. With a record of 16-4, he stood a giant five foot eleven and was entering his sophomore fight in the WEC. It was going to be the toughest opponent of my career.

The event took place at *Palms Casino* in Las Vegas and was broadcast live on *Versus Television*. The headline bout was UFC standout Donald Cerrone, and celebrities packed the arena. Despite being the first time I was under so much pressure, and with the biggest lights of the sport beating down on me, I couldn't wait to get in the cage! And it showed. The fight was a one-sided affair. I landed heavy strikes and a few big slams and pounded my way to a triumphant victory by unanimous decision.

It was by far the single most defining moment of my life so far. Winning that fight put my name in the headlines. I was then ranked number twenty-two in the world by *fightmatrix.com*. Sponsors started paying me to do appearances. I secured a radio endorsement deal and even traveled back to Japan to help train and corner Rumina Sato for his Shoot fight against top-ranked Ryota Matsune (which Rumina won by second-round TKO).

To most athletes, this would have been exactly what they wanted. Only I was still battling my own demons of imposter syndrome. Deep down, I didn't believe I belonged there. The years of self-doubt and sabotage made me feel like a phony, no matter what successes I may have had.

FUN SIDE STORY

In the fight world, promoters always ask, "Who do you want to fight next?"

After I won my debut, I was asked that very question. My response was a kid who was new to the show, just like me, Demetrius Johnson. The organization didn't like the match-up. Apparently, I was too strong of a wrestler for him at the time. Whether true or not, I took the victory in my head. Little did I know, the guy I wanted to fight would later become the most dominant UFC flyweight champion in the sport's history! Anyway, for that fight, another name was offered.

SELF-REFLECTION / CREATING A SUPERHERO

The idea of failing scares us. I get it. But what are we actually afraid of? I can tell you unashamedly that I have been afraid of almost everything. When I started fighting, I was constantly terrified of it. I was afraid of getting hurt. I was afraid of losing. I was afraid my opponent was better than me. My past pains had caused me to fail over and over again. I honestly didn't know how to handle the emotions. The self-image that I had at the time was shaky and not strong enough to be a truly formidable fighter. So, I created a character in my mind that was.

It might sound crazy to most people, but it worked. I just

needed a trigger to unleash that ferocious alter ego. Something that would transform me from Bruce Banner to Hulk. And so, for every fight, I chose a funky hairstyle. That was my trigger. It let me become something bigger and overcome the limiting beliefs I held about myself. I would transform into "THE SAVAGE." That would transform my fights and allow me to build a formidable name and a following to match.

Over the years, that character led my path from fighting in the first-ever legally sanctioned events in California to winning championship titles.

My alter ego gave me the opportunity to travel around the world and eventually fight for the biggest shows in the sport... there was only one problem. In my mind, The SAVAGE was just a character. And that character was about to get a rude wake-up call.

WE ALL HAVE BAD DAYS

 "No matter what comes your way, just don't let it phase you; you can overcome anything."

— ROSE NAMAJUNAS

* * *

Let's face it, losing sucks. I'm sure we can all agree on that. We don't celebrate defeat... especially if it involves getting humiliated on national television in front of millions of people. That *really* sucks.

I remember getting the call during practice.

My coach sat me down and said, "We have our next opponent."

But something seemed off. It was almost as if he was afraid

to tell me who it was. Now, given my history of self-confidence issues, that definitely didn't help. He paused, then said, "It's Scott Jorgensen." If you don't already know, Scott was a straight-up *killer* in the division at the time. I believe he was actually ranked among the top five in the world, and for a good reason. Every fight he was in had been a *Fight of the Night* candidate, and he was always in a championship title conversation (in fact, he did eventually fight for the title).

If I wanted to go toe to toe with the best in the world, well, that was my opportunity. Most people have to wait much longer to get a chance like it. If I beat him, I would be one step closer to becoming an actual world champion! How crazy would that be? I was literally weeks away from savoring a moment that I had dreamed about. All I needed to do was avoid letting the idea of who he was psych me out. I would also need to train my ass off and prove that I belonged in that fight.

During the eight-week camp that followed, we prepared for every possible scenario. I was ready to shock the world. When the betting predictions came out, they had me down as a seven-to-one underdog… which was understandable. But I didn't care about those odds. I was ready to beat the monster that would stand before me. As we arrived at the arena and began warming up, we went over my game plan one last time. My coaches and I knew what we were there to do. It was time to deliver some shock and awe to the world. I had all the tools at my disposal to beat him. I just had to be careful not to lose to myself.

COLUMBUS, OHIO

The fight took place in Columbus, Ohio. I remember everything as clear as yesterday. There I was, standing behind the curtain, anxiously waiting to hear my music so I could walk the long tunnel down to the cage and take him down. Finally, the wait was over.

I heard the call from legendary Burt Watson, "It's time to roll, baby. Let's go, Chad! Time to walk!"

Energy surged through me. The crowd roared. The ground shook beneath my feet. The music vibrated through my entire body. I moved past the curtain and into the arena. Then it happened. A heatwave struck me. I felt the energy of the ten thousand people in attendance banging on the floor and clapping their hands. Electricity ran through me. It almost felt like an out-of-body experience. My excitement melted into fear. With each step toward the cage, I became increasingly less focused and more terrified. The crowd had beat me. The pressure was breaking me, and then it clicked, *oh shit, I'm about to fight Scott Jorgensen!*

Our game plan was simple—make him box with me. Don't shoot at him. Get him frustrated. Pick him apart on the feet. As the cage door closed, I had already forgotten the plan. That is probably not the best way to start a fight, especially with such an incredibly dangerous guy. The bell sounded. I bounced around. At forty-six seconds in, I went for a takedown that was set up horribly. Scott grabbed my neck, pushed me into the cage, and lifted me off the floor in a strangle as my feet dangled in the air. That would later be called a "death choke" by the media, as it ended up putting me to sleep in just under a minute... on national TV and in front of millions of people. I'd done it again. I'd let my fear of the unknown affect the outcome before the contest even got fully underway. I'd proven all the doubters right.

Once the fight was over, my walk of shame to the locker room felt like a marathon. I was completely embarrassed. I wanted to burst into tears. When I finally arrived backstage, I just broke down. Every repressed emotion that had been bottled up for years came to the surface all at once. In my mind, that loss was the biggest failure of my life. And it wasn't just me. My boxing coach was so upset that he immediately left the arena. It was the *worst*. He was so disappointed in me that I didn't see him again until we got back to Los Angeles.

I was heartbroken. I was discouraged. But not because I lost. It was because I'd been the victim of my own bullshit. Again, I felt sorry for myself. I made every excuse as to why it happened. The more I focused on the fight, the deeper I sunk into depression. I didn't want to train or be around people, and I especially didn't want to see footage of the damn fight. Every time it came up, the painful cycle of emotions bulldozed me all over again. It was a waking nightmare.

As days passed, it only got worse. Then came a day when I just wanted to grab a burger by myself at a favorite local spot. While waiting for my order, an old client saw me sitting at the table. He and his son walked over and asked me how the fight went. Thankfully, they hadn't seen it. *What a relief!* I explained that it didn't go my way but that I would bounce back from the loss. We shook hands, and they went back to their table. Now, what happened next is something that only happens in the movies.

I heard a voice from across the restaurant yell, "Hey, Chad, look! You're on TV!"

I looked up from my table and saw that he was right. All of the TVs above the bar were showing the WEC, and it just happened to be my fight. *You have GOT to be fucking kidding me.* Now, since he yelled it across the room, everyone there immediately knew it was me. I smiled and put my head down as I finished my sad burger.

So, clearly, things were looking a little rough for me. I wasn't really training, had allowed my diet to turn to shit, and was gaining a ton of weight. It wasn't until I saw a family photo that I realized the sorry state I was in. I didn't even recognize myself. But my pity party kept rocking for a few more months. Every time the WEC played or Scott was mentioned, the now-infamous choke was as well. Hell, internet trolls continued sending me clips on Twitter for almost two years after the fight!

At a certain point, I just couldn't take it anymore. I reached my breaking point. That's when I snapped. That's when I said to myself, "You need to get over this and stop being a little bitch!" And that's when I realized—while sitting there, moping around —that I was missing the big picture and needed to start giving myself more credit for fighting on the biggest stage in the world. Who else can say that? Who else has had that opportunity? Who else has earned their place there? I had, same as all those other elite fighters. It was time to start giving myself credit. Time to cut the bullshit I was feeding myself. *So, you had a bad day... get over it.* Failing is part of the process. The path to success is not a smooth one.

As soon as I finally accepted that, my life honestly began to change. I stopped running from challenges. I no longer questioned myself. Instead, I began believing that all the bad days served a purpose. Adversity does not teach us the lessons we want but the ones we need. Nothing great comes for free.

10

NO STORM LASTS FOREVER

 "When the storm rips you to pieces, you get to decide how to put yourself back together again."

— BRYANT H. MCGILL

* * *

I t's no secret that I'm a bit of a comic book nerd. Even my son is named Logan, after the Wolverine from X-Men. The storylines of superheroes have always resonated with me—especially those of characters who were molded out of some type of adversity. And even more so, those about heroes who finally decide that it is time to stop giving in to what was scaring them, emerge from the shadows, and stand up to their fear. To be perfectly clear, doing that doesn't mean that they were no longer afraid. Instead, it means that they realized it was time to stop running away from the things that were terrifying them.

Over the years, I have realized that fear is the biggest enemy of progress. Sometimes we surround ourselves with unrealistic fears or false, limiting beliefs that prevent us from pursuing our goals and desires. They keep us from doing important things like getting our dream job, making important life decisions, or finding the right type of relationship. Often, we normalize carrying those fears in our hearts so much so that they impede our ability to pursue what we really want in life. Many of us become crippled and overwhelmed by fears of not being capable enough of accomplishing goals. I want to tell you that these are just illusions. They have *no* grounding in real life. You may have started to believe in concepts that are baseless and incorrect. But if you take the time to look around, you'll see that the most successful people are the ones who have challenged those misconceptions. They have the ability to monitor and analyze their beliefs logically. They never let their fears become a barrier between them and their goals.

I believe that we all walk around with some sort of doubt in our minds. There is not a single person on earth who has never felt fear. Even the people who seem unbreakable possess insecurities. Everyone struggles at some point in life. The only difference between us is found in how we react to those experiences. Some play the victim; others rise to the occasion.

Now I truly mean it when I say I have tried everything to reprogram my brain. Really. Everything from meditating and practicing daily note-taking and goal writing to working with mental sports coaches, NLP (neuro-linguistic programming) coaches, and hypnotherapists. Seriously, I've tried everything. I found the answer. Turns out it was all me. The only thing that stopped me from reaching my goals was me. My own mind. I had fallen victim to crazy assumptions about myself that didn't even bear the slightest resemblance to the truth.

"Whether you think you can or you think you can't. Your right."

— HENRY FORD

* * *

There are moments in life when we go through sudden or unpredictable changes. Moments when our psyche takes over in an attempt to overwrite reality with a plausible story to protect us from the pain of that reality. We begin absorbing other people's opinions instead of forming our own. The judgments of others start molding the way we deal with challenges, and as a result, we lose the ability to strive forward. This forms a self-destructive path that crystalizes with each passing day and becomes harder and harder to break. The stories in our heads stop us from reaching our true potential. We have to learn from our mistakes and not let the negative dialogue about them influence our future.

After I lost the fight to Scott Jorgensen, it was clear that I needed to make some significant internal changes. THE SAVAGE didn't need a new outrageous hairstyle; I didn't need the pushed image. I realized that all this time, THE SAVAGE had been holding me back.

I had been hiding behind a persona that was created to give me strength, but it was actually doing the opposite. All my false beliefs and insecurities had to be addressed head-on. I could no longer hide. It started with shaving off the mohawk. It was time to drop the facade and see who I really was, time to give birth to a new chapter of my journey.

I began journaling. I wrote my daily victories and losses. I wrote short-term and long-term goals. I wanted to keep track of my achievements and celebrate even the smallest wins. This was one of the most remarkable techniques and one that helped immensely. Day by day, my vision started growing. And before I knew it, a month had passed. I noticed an unbelievable amount of energy that drew me even closer to my goals each day. Every time I wrote, it was like seeing the day again on replay. There was excitement every time I pulled my notepad out. It became my new secret weapon for learning about myself and is something I still do religiously to this day.

My journey started with accepting all my inner fears, which was a necessary step to take before I could really overcome them or ultimately eliminate them from my life. As they say, acceptance is the first step! Doing that was one of the biggest changes I needed to make. I realized that there was no point in denying that fear was something we all experience. Many of us, at least on some level, view confident people as simply not being afraid… but let's get real here—deep down, we are all afraid of something. We are fearful of failure. We are afraid of acceptance. We are even scared of succeeding, as odd as that sounds.

Eventually, my confidence began to grow. That's when the doubts started getting quieter and quieter. My actions began to change. The way I spoke and carried myself was changing as well. I began researching self-development and sports psychology, all while listening to and reading success stories of other athletes and entrepreneurs I admired.

I began absorbing information like a sponge. Soaking up all that information was like gassing up with high-octane fuel for developing an obsession with becoming more self-aware. I began to pay special attention to my thoughts and actions. Words like *maybe, can't,* and *try,* began to look like limiting beliefs and were entirely removed from my vocabulary.

Over time, my head started to clear up. The clouds in my mind softened, and training became fun again. For the first time in as long as I could remember, I was genuinely happy. My history of self-doubt was fueled by the internal dialog stemming from how I talked to myself when alone. The lessons I was learning during that process were monumental.

LESSON # 1: I WAS NOT MADE OF GLASS.

I could take a punch. In fact, I think EVERYONE should get hit in the face at least once to see how strong they really are.

Mike Tyson said it best: *"Everyone has a plan until they get hit in the face."*

Sometimes, when we are stubborn, this lesson may need a few extra reminders to really sink in. Such is life. It's going to make things ugly, and when it does, we have to be ready.

LESSON # 2: I SEEMED TO BE GOOD AT THIS FIGHTING THING.

Even though EVERY event had me absolutely terrified, there was a power inside me begging to be set free. My experience made me realize that we live in a world of illusions, of curated exteriors, where we often do not get a chance to form an accurate image of ourselves or others. Our fears mislead us in many ways. They instill in us the insecurities that tell us that we are not good enough.

It took me years to realize the simple mistake I had been making. The solution was to keep my focus on progress and not look past the present moment.

LESSON # 3: I HAD NOTHING TO PROVE TO ANYONE ELSE EXCEPT MYSELF.

The approval of others is something many of us crave. We want to be liked; we want to fit in. But at what cost?

As soon as I became my number one fan, everything changed. I stopped seeking the approval of others and focused solely on my own actions. The only person I was in competition with was myself. Every day was a chance to push further, to reach higher, to get better. The only validation I needed was knowing that I'd put in the work.

A few months passed, and I had been training hard. I wanted to test myself. I needed to know if this was all bullshit or if I was finally starting to get it. My next challenge would be the exact test I needed. Not just because of who my opponent was but because of all the trials that I was about to face.

When my next fight was announced, I had a long twelve weeks to prepare for it. That was a luxury because, in most cases, you only have four to six weeks at most to prepare. Training camp started, and I had just moved into a new condo with a now ex-girlfriend. That's when I met Andre. I'll talk more about him later.

My opponent was a Chuck Liddell student and protégé, Antonio Banuelos. Antonio was another killer. At the time, he had already fought for the WEC title and had more fights in the promotion than any other bantamweight. But that wasn't the only big news. The UFC had just announced that they would officially be moving all bantamweights to their roaster after the upcoming event. The winner would face Miguel Torres in the very first UFC one hundred- and thirty-five-pound bout.

The old me wanted to be afraid. However, with the passage of time, I realized that I had a choice. I could become my own superhero. Nobody was going to hand me my dreams. I had to chase them for myself, and at some point, I would need to slay the monster that was hiding under the bed to do that.

As the days passed, my entire attitude started to transform. I could feel the burning desire to win building inside me. There was a confidence that was brand new. Every time the doubts entered my mind, I trained even harder. You weren't going to outwork me. Not possible. I was becoming a *machine;* from the start of the day right through to the very end. My routines were carefully planned.

7 A.M. - Running

8 A.M. – Opening the gym & teaching group class

9 A.M. – Teaching private clients

10-11 A.M. – Boxing/strength & conditioning

12 P.M. – MMA training

4-6 P.M. – Teaching private clients

6 P.M. – Teaching group class and running the gym

8 P.M. – Jiu-Jitsu training

My days were ticking precisely like clockwork. I loved every bit of the grind. In fact, I couldn't get enough of it. But as the fight got closer, things began to change. And when they did, they did fast.

Being born with scoliosis and enduring years of contact sports is a top-shelf cocktail recipe for disaster. It was my coach's job to always push me and find new ways of going beyond my limits. In a routine strength and conditioning session, my entire world shifted. I was near the end of a session and was attempting to do a deadlift and press with a bar that had no weight on it. It should have been something a kid could do. Being lazy and tired, I yanked the bar from the floor with terrible form. Instantly, two lightning bolts shot down my leg. I dropped to the ground.

Over the next few days, the pain intensified. Without insurance, I was unable to get an MRI or X-ray to see what was going on. Luckily, A doctor friend of mine was able to give me a cortisone injection for the pain. It was heaven. In a few days, I was feeling back to normal. The Savage was temporarily running full speed ahead, like nothing ever happened. Little did I know that this was just the beginning.

In general, fighting is a very selfish sport. Most people will never understand what goes into it, not unless they have actually been through it themselves. I hear some variation of this all the time, "Must be nice to just work out all day," or the best one, "You're lucky. I have to work for a living." Both of these are so far from the truth; it's disgusting.

A professional athlete's life is plagued with tension, body pain, extreme dieting, and stress. For fighters, this is also combined with a countdown for a date with someone who wants to punch your head in! These difficulties tend to stretch well beyond just the fight.

Deep into camp, my relationship had been rocky. Now, that wasn't uncommon for us—the constant build-up of emotions is never easy on anyone's relationship—but as the event drew closer, my focus was becoming more and more important, and that tension was really sapping it.

Instead of enduring the daily arguing at home, I decided to leave for a few days and stay with a buddy to clear my mind. However, that was easier said than done! Two nights in, my car was broken into. The window was shattered, and all my training gear was stolen. To make it worse, the car was parked on the street and stuck in the middle of a massive rainstorm. My only option? Go back home. I called my partner to let her know what was happening but had no response. Earlier that day, she had mentioned leaving to have dinner with a friend. I hadn't thought anything of it.

As the rain intensified, everything on the inside of my car got soaked. The plan was simple—jump in the driver's seat, head to the house, drop off any remaining stuff, and leave. But hey, I should have known... nothing is ever "simple" in my story. The garage opened, and to my surprise, her car was inside. *Weird.* She was not supposed to be home.

Now I may have been developing my inner superhero at the time... and that superhero was not Spiderman, but some kind of spidey sense within me began to tingle. Something felt off. I should have turned around and left, but I didn't. Instead, I walked to the garage door. Surprisingly, it was locked. We never locked that door. *Strange.* That was another opportunity for me to leave. But again, I didn't.

Deep down, it was clear what would be coming next. My adrenaline began to pump as I walked through the pouring rain and through the front door of the house. Before I could put the key in, she opened it. Looking at me with fear, she began apologizing. Her face turned red as tears came tumbling down it.

A real nightmare had come true. There was another man in our bedroom. Everything inside me wanted to rip him apart. The coward had locked himself in the bathroom and refused to show his face. I banged and kicked on the door, trying to lure him out. He must have been curled in the fetal position, rocking back in forth, hoping I never got in. Lucky for him, I didn't.

To this day, I don't know who it was. To be honest, it doesn't really matter anyways. I still had the fight to worry about, and at that moment was presented with another obstacle. A cheating girlfriend and, in turn, homeless again.

The fight was only a few weeks away. I didn't have time to find a place or even worry about the situation. I did the only thing I could think of, and that was to move into the gym. There's a common expression among people who want to make serious gains, *"You must live in the gym,"* and well, I did just that. No home, no girlfriend, no distractions. I was pure focus. Each time I felt emotions getting to me, I would channel them into another training session. Those obstacles became advantages. Time flew by, and before I knew it, we were headed to Denver to make the final preparations.

Sitting at fifty-three hundred feet up, the elevation of a mile-high city was going to take a few days to get acclimated to. Because of that, to ensure we had every advantage possible, we arrived a week early. I stayed with a buddy who had a fighter house that was designed for high-altitude training. On our first day, I went for a long run and made stair sprints up a giant mountain... probably not the smartest thing to do when you are not used to the thin air! But I still did it. That night, I laid on the floor throwing up, my head spinning due to altitude sickness.

That was my first time ever experiencing training at such an elevation. In the beginning, it felt like I couldn't breathe—like I was a fish out of water—and whenever I worked out, it was as if I was being suffocated in between rounds. Luckily, as the days wore on, my body started to get used to the thin air. Everything finally started to click into place. It was perfect timing, as Chang Sung Jung (The Korean Zombie) had just shown up for training. We finished our camp together. It was amazing. The machine was back.

With sixteen fights now under my belt, I thought I had weight cutting down. Ho-ly-shit... was I wrong! The cut I did next was absolutely terrible. For five hours, I was dressed in plastics and sweats, attempting to drain my body of all its water and remove the nine pounds that I was still overweight by. We rotated between sauna, treadmill, and lying on the floor while covered in towels. The elevation made the normal vertigo that comes with dehydration feel *insane*. The more weight came off, the dizzier I felt. It made me sick to my core. I got to the point where I couldn't even walk. I felt like I was dying, but I made it. Finally, the hard part was over. My weight was down to the class limit of one hundred and thirty-five pounds. Nothing in the world had the power to stop me!

I entered the sold-out arena of 6500 fans. Jose Aldo— arguably the greatest featherweight of all time—headlined the event. I stared across the cage at Antonio Banuelos with a burning eagerness to fight in my eyes, and he glared back at me with the same intensity. I knew this was going to be a war, and I was ready for it! We exchanged punches and kicks for most of the round. As the clock approached the final 30 seconds, he took me down, and then it all started. I secured a sneaky D'arce choke from the bottom position. It was one of my favorite strangles. I squeezed and knew I only had a few seconds to finish it. HE TAPPED!

I let go of the submission as the sound of the bell rang at the end of the round. The fight was over, or so I thought. It turned out the referee did not see the tap. Because I let go, he assumed the round had ended! However, the fight continued. This was the point where good coaching was needed. I was confused, stressed, and my adrenaline had been dumped. Instead of trying to get my mind and body back into the fight, my corner spent the break arguing with each other about what needed to happen. That was how the second round began, with me still having no clue what adjustments were needed. To make things worse, all I could hear was my corner continuing to yell over each other. Nothing made sense. Not at all. This was not how things were supposed to be. During a fight, a fighter's mind is in a state of chaos. We need calm and clearly directed commands to help us navigate properly. The third round was more of the same. I would lose by the majority decision. Two rounds to one. I would also lose my opportunity to fight on the first-ever UFC bantamweight card.

Everything I had sacrificed—all the blood, every last drop of blood and sweat—none of it mattered at all. I tried to find a reason for why it'd happened. I had given up everything. I had nothing left in me to give. Why did I keep doing this to myself? Every time I got close, something always happened that made it get ripped away from me. It was at that moment it all clicked… it's because I am a fighter! I built my life this way. This is what we do; we fight. Whether we win or lose, we get up, we get back on our feet, and we do it again.

WHEN OPPORTUNITY KNOCKS

Losing the fight and my opportunity to be on the first UFC bantamweight card was a tough pill to swallow. Instead of making excuses, I had to get back in the gym and start rebuilding. All of the WEC contracts were merged into the parent company—Zuffa. I was now a UFC fighter. At least on paper. My name was on the online roster and UFC website. The matchmakers contacted me about staying ready as they were figuring out fights and how the new division was going to roll out. So, I waited… and waited. After about six months of waiting and training my ass off, I still had not heard anything of a potential fight.

The promotion had already hosted several events, and I was not included in any. But that wasn't the worst thing. My back was really starting to give me problems again, and I was in need of another cortisone shot. Each day it was getting harder and harder to simply get out of bed. The only option I had was to get back to the doctor and seek another injection.

I did that. With the pain again temporarily relieved, I was given permission to fight outside of the UFC. I just couldn't afford to lose. We took a fairly safe fight, and I would win by first-round submission. I hoped it would lead to a fight for me on the big stage, and eventually.

It did, just not the fight I expected.

U.S.A. VS. NEW ZEALAND

While the UFC was still giving me the run-around, I had an amazing opportunity arise—a new international event called *The Cage*. It would be held in New Zealand, and they were looking for American fighters to represent the U.S.A. I was offered a spot and accepted. My opponent would be a young kickboxer who was making big waves in his native land. His name was *Kai Kara France*. The name may sound familiar and with good reason. Kai is now one of the top three ranked UFC flyweights in the world (In fact, he has even fought for the flyweight world title). This was a great opportunity. I knew that beating the New Zealand champ was not going to be easy. Anytime you travel to someone else's backyard, you are not being brought there to win. Oddly, I was extremely excited. Not just to represent my country but because I really wanted the challenge of facing another nation's best fighter.

After a thirteen-hour flight, we finally arrived in Auckland. Once we landed, we still had another three-and-a-half-hour car ride to the small fishing town called *Whakatane*. Let me tell you, that place was *stunning*. It was as if we'd arrived in a hidden world. Pulling up to the venue, we were met by a line of native Maori who greeted all the athletes with a warrior's Haka ceremonial dance. While I had seen a Haka performed on TV, I'd never been privileged enough to experience one in person.

It was extremely powerful—you could feel the energy running through them as they pummeled the ground and yelled. It immediately felt like we were there for war. One of the things that also stood out to me was the sense of family. By five in the afternoon, the entire town would turn off. Businesses all shut down, and families gathered together outside. This collective spirit was very apparent from the moment we arrived until we left. They had unity, which was something that I gravitated to. Even though they were of warrior ancestry, they were together. My time with the Maori may have sparked the sense of community that I project onto my athletes today.

Going into the fight, I was oddly calm and, at the same time, super excited despite the fact I was facing such a tough opponent. My goal was just to embrace the present. After all, who gives a fuck about the pressure!

'I'm in a different country.
I'm fighting their champion.
I have nothing to lose.
Just go fight.'

That night, my stomach was pissed. I probably ate too many banoffee pies—amongst the many other delicious foods that are not advisable to consume before a fight—and so didn't get much sleep. Instead, I spent most of the later hours vomiting my brains out.

The morning arrived, and I started the day with my coffee (a flat white) and a conversation with a local who wanted to remind me that the Maori had been cannibals only one hundred years ago. That's not something you want to hear as you're getting ready to battle one in a few hours! However, I still felt no pressure. Only a visceral excitement to fight.

Just the fact that I was there for the event was a win to me, despite my tenure ending with the WEC. You could tell that the crowd was ready for a spectacle. As the show started, they had Harley-Davidsons in the arena that circled the cage and roared their engines. I had never seen anything like that before an event, and I still haven't to this day. That set the atmosphere for the audience and the fighters.

Finally, it was time for the fight to get underway. I pressed forward on Kai, and we exchanged a few strikes. Then I finally got the takedown. There was no question about what each of our game plans were to be—a wrestler versus a striker. He didn't want to be on the ground with me, and in most people's eyes, I didn't want to stand with him. After I took him down, he got back up, and I remember thinking, *Shit*. It was going to be *that* kind of a fight. However, as the fight wore on, I noticed something. I would change levels, and so would Kai. I would drop, and he would drop. It was almost like he was mirroring me. *Wait a minute,* I told myself, *He's following me.* Once I realized what was happening, I decided to go for a big shot. I was going to fake my level change, then load an uppercut to meet him on the bounce.

I dropped down. He took the bait, allowing me to throw a shot that landed right on his chin. I hit him so hard that his feet lifted off of the canvas. As soon as he hit the ground, I jumped on him and unloaded with strikes landing at least twenty unanswered shots before the ref finally jumped in. I won by first-round knockout. One of the things I realized after winning was that I could strike with the best in the world. That I'm not just a *Jiu-Jitsu* guy, not just a grappler, and that I'd just proved it.

After the fight, we were treated like kings. First, a private helicopter tour of the island, and then a full-blown celebration with the townspeople. We drank, we sang, we bonded over the culture, and were again treated to a closed-door Haka. That night it was said by someone that I must have Maori blood in me with the way that I fought. You could tell they were genuinely happy to have me there, as was I. It made me feel like a part of them. It was an experience of a lifetime. I honestly didn't want to go home. However, after another thirteen-hour flight, I was back in the States. The brutal combination of traveling and fighting made my back feel unbearable. There was a stabbing pain that ran from my lower back down to my hip and all the way down to my foot. Up until then, I had been surviving on cortisone shots. Doctors had told me that over time my body would build a tolerance, and the injections would no longer work. I was only masking the pain, and I knew that eventually, it would all catch up to me… and guess what? It did.

11

BACK SURGERY

 "Challenge yourself every day to do better and be better. Remember, growth starts with a decision to move beyond your present circumstances."

— **ROBERT TEW**

very athlete pushes through injuries. It might be hard for a common person to relate to our everyday struggles when coping with bumps and bruises, but for a fighter? Well, that's just a regular day at the office.

Each round brings with it the potential for sustaining lasting injuries that you'll feel for the rest of your life. Sure, sometimes it's just a muscle sprain or a cut. But other days, the resulting pain may inhibit our ability to even get out of bed in the morning. Sometimes it can last for days. But, when it's all said and done, that's how fighting works. Every fighter that plays this game knows the risk involved. They also know that as long as you are following your passion and chasing your dream, all the pain is worth it.

In wrestling, we used to joke that tape would fix everything. Broke a finger? Tape it! Got a cut? Tape it. Did your shoulder just pop out? Oh, let's tape it! There was even one fight when I actually did break my finger in the middle of practice. I taped it up and continued on. However, there are still some injuries that magical tape won't fix. The real bad ones.

Throughout my athletic career, I have suffered every injury that you can think of, from cuts, stitches, and fractures to terrifying infections. I have experienced it all. Although those decades of damage have had a significant impact on my physical health, I am still grateful for every pain. Each one has made me a stronger person—mentally and emotionally. In the upcoming chapters, I'm going to run through a detailed list of the injuries I have acquired throughout my journey. These are my dues that have been paid. And the lingering pain is the interest accrued.

We're going to start with the most significant, one that even a tough mind could not push past. It was my back.

Throughout my life, I have had to deal with agonizing back problems. There have been days when getting up from the couch seemed impossible. Every minute felt like an hour. The excruciating pain often made me wonder why I was born this way. My scoliosis sometimes made simple, everyday chores a herculean challenge.

As a kid, I used to struggle during school as well. There was a phase when the doctors had me wear one of those embarrassing back braces under my clothes to try and help re-align my spine as I grew.

In my early teens was when doctors talked to my parents about surgery—rods that were going to be put straight into my spine. As horrific as it sounds, thankfully, I never had to go through with it. Luckily for me, my growth spurt didn't come until after high school. At which point, the constant training I'd been doing had naturally built muscles around my back and core. However, given that I was living with scoliosis, a lifetime of wrestling, and years of wear and tear, well… it had all been gradually adding up. That balance would come due. As my fighting career intensified, so did my back issues.

One cortisone shot turned into multiple doses every few months. The issues I had been masking were going to come barreling down on me later, but the fear of needing long-term treatment kept me from getting an actual diagnosis.

Ignoring it was made easy by focusing so intensely on something else. Training. Nothing came above training, especially not a potentially time-consuming procedure. Besides, the shots had been working! They were a quick remedy to the pain that put me right back into training mode. Ignorance is bliss, at least for a while.

Eventually, the inevitable happened. The shots stopped working. All the doctor's concerns were explained to me early on. I didn't listen. The cortisone was never meant to be a long-term fix. As predicted, over time, its effectiveness did wear down. As my next fight approached, my pain reached an all-time high.

With the cortisone no longer a viable option, I took my first epidural—for those fortunate enough not to know what that is, it's a shot directly into the spine. My options were running out, and time was not on my side.

TESTING THE LIMITS

So yeah, my back was a mess. With the opportunity to fight, the name Joe Soto also came along. Joe was one of the biggest names in MMA that wasn't in the UFC. He had just finished a run in Bellator, where he was the inaugural Featherweight Champion. My fight with Joe was with a version of him that'd just come back from a severe eye injury (detached retina) that many thought would've meant the end of his career.

Before having the chance to fight him, the UFC had basically told me that if I beat a guy of this caliber, that will guarantee me a spot back on the UFC roster. So, it was a golden opportunity for me to prove myself. All eyes were on us.

Turning down this fight was not an option. My condition didn't matter. The champion inside me said that I could beat him. However, despite being incredibly motivated and determined, I was nervous about the situation. Then it got worse. The epidural stopped working. I was running on sheer willpower. There wasn't going to be much of a training camp. I couldn't wrestle, and Joe was one of the greatest grapplers in the world. I had to adapt my training in a manner that would help me protect my back. That was the biggest challenge. I knew that another injury to it could be catastrophic. Surprisingly, going into the fight, I actually felt pretty good. I had confidence in my wrestling defense and my footwork, so I knew I had a chance at winning just as long as I kept Soto off of me.

The first round went well. I stopped several takedowns, and my back was holding up great. In the second, I was even more confident because my game plan was working. But then it finally happened—Joe was able to secure a takedown. I managed to get back up on my feet, but he took me down again. I couldn't get him off me, and I felt my body give out. That led to him taking my back and securing a rear-naked choke that actually put me to sleep. I was devastated, but I knew going into it that this fight was going to test my body's limitations and that I'd find out if it either could or couldn't take it. It could not. Joe would later fight for the UFC bantamweight title, while I would have a different battle on my hands.

The following day, I was unable to get out of bed. It was my first time feeling what would be the beginning of the worst pain of my life. I later found out it was due to a damaged sciatic nerve resulting from extremely herniated discs in my back.

Over the years, I had trained as if I had never had an injury. Now, that was partially due to the fact that, like most fighters, I didn't have health insurance. I truly believed in the concept of 'mind over matter'… especially when it came to pain. In truth, I was just masking it all with cortisone and epidural injections. I ignorantly denied the fact that I needed to take care of the injury and seek proper treatment.

My battle against the herniated disks had caused severe sciatic pain that ran down my hip and into my foot. If you haven't ever experienced it, then I hope you never do. The pain was so violent that every day felt like an absolute nightmare. I couldn't even stand up straight. So just sit down then, right? Well, sitting down for more than five minutes at a time would cause a knife-like sensation in my hip and leg. Getting out of bed was a forty-five-minute ordeal. I would sit up, then proceed to fall back down due to the excruciating pain. Each attempt was spent arguing with myself using encouraging words, like "Stop being a pussy and just get up."

I was completely miserable, depressed, and accepting of defeat. The time had come when I had no other option than to seek a specialist to see what could be done.

It wasn't long after that I found myself in doctor's office after doctor's office. Each gave an opinion about my situation. All of them, after reviewing my MRI scans, wanted to open me up. Not a single one recommended rehab or therapy to try and negate the need for surgery. In fact, one doctor was actually surprised that I was able to walk in there to see them! When he took a look at the MRI, he was certain that the person coming into his office that day was going to be in a wheelchair.

The size of my herniation was unheard of for someone that

was not only walking but had just competed and won a world championship Jiu-Jitsu event. Later, the same doctor ended up using my scans in a clinical study after being so amazed by seeing anyone so active with such a large herniation.

The average person who complains of back pain might have a slight bulge of two to three millimeters. Once the disc extends between a four to six range, doctors will recommend seeing a specialist and therapy. Now, that's on the milder but still painful end. Once the herniations reach the seven-to-nine-millimeter range, surgery is recommended. Mine was a *twelve-millimeter herniation*. I was a mess, but something still didn't sit right with me that not a single doctor even wanted to try therapy before slicing my back open.

They'd say things like, *"Oh, it's such an easy procedure now. We go in, cut out the bad stuff, and send you off."*

It sounded so simple. But what they forgot—or neglected—to mention was that any kind of surgery is a major event. If anything goes wrong, it's a big deal. I understood how bad my situation was. However, all the doctors had already assumed what I was doing in my career was impossible. So, it stood to reason that maybe there was something else they were missing or could be done. I refused to accept that surgery was my only option. I needed to do more research on my own.

After meeting with my rehab team at OC Fight Docs, the owner and head of therapy—Ron Kessler—wanted me to get one more opinion. Dr. Justin Paquett is who we called. Paquette gave off this young playboy-type vibe, with a leather jacket over his scrubs, a coffee in one hand, and my MRI scans in the other. I remember that he asked me about the injury and what the other doctors had said. What he did next was something that I didn't expect.

He threw my MRIs away and said he doesn't work with injuries based on the opinions of others and that he needs to make his own assessments first. This was the first doctor to offer therapy before committing to full-blown back surgery. We agreed on following a six-month plan. If that rehab didn't work, then we would consider the next step. People thought I was crazy. I was getting messages from family, friends, and even doctors who I had previously seen, all telling me that I was only making it worse and that I needed to start thinking about what to do next in my career.

Everyone was convinced that my fighting days were over. There was one message that stood out to me more than any other.

"You had a great career; there's no shame in hanging it up."

I was very much ready to accept whatever the future held for me. But not without a fight.

THE WATERMELON SEED

Dr. Paquett was the only specialist that suggested we exhaust all our options before thinking about surgery. That would ease the decision-making process if and when that time was to come. The rehab was all about exercises that would help strengthen the muscles around my lumbar and hopefully help push the discs back into place in the process. Most of the time, therapy like that would be for smaller herniations. The doctors' used an analogy of a watermelon seed, saying that every time they tried to push the seed back into place through exercises, the compression of the disks would squeeze the flat squishy seed back out. This became very frustrating because it made it seem like progress was limited.

As soon as we made steps forward, it would then be gone. This caused a battle with real depression and the looming fear of never being able to compete again. Every day was an internal struggle, a desperate fight against slipping into a dark place.

After the six months of therapy were up, the original doctors' assumptions were correct. I needed surgery. The rehab had not worked. And the longer we waited, the worse it was going to get. The procedure that we ended up doing was a *microdiscectomy*—which involved cutting off the segment of a disk that was pinching the nerve. We would also do stem cell injections, from the marrow of my hip, into the surgery points to create a faster healing process and hopefully regenerate the fluid in the disks.

After the surgery, Dr. Paquett told me that my sciatic nerve was so damaged that it looked like it had been in a dogfight. The extent of the injury would also most likely mean residual pain symptoms for the rest of my life.

RECOVERY

Twenty-four hours after the surgery, I had already been discharged. My road to recovery had begun. I was overwhelmed with the fear of damaging my back again. I had to regain confidence in every physical movement, starting with how to walk. Then came squatting and, eventually, weight-bearing movements. Mastering each exercise took two to three months before I was allowed to move on to the next. As we progressed, my confidence started to build, and the fear of throwing out my back started to fade. I found myself constantly trying to push my limits in order to recover more quickly.

By month six, I was almost fully recovered. By the eighth month mark, I was back to full training and really wanted to see what kind of shape I was in. So, I said fuck it and did something absolutely insane. I took a fight. Nine months out of surgery, I was back in the cage. I fought Cody Gibson – another one of the toughest fighters outside of the UFC. We had a back-and-forth first round, and I nearly finished him twice. Then I made one glaring mistake and ended up getting caught with a guillotine choke. Losing sucks. But nine months prior, I was battling the worst pain in my life. Doctors said I would never fight again. Yet there I was, proving them all wrong. I was already winning. I just needed time to rebuild my body properly and then see how far I could truly go. (Cody later signed with the UFC).

OCCUPATION FIGHTER

12

"Fighting is not what I do – it's who I am. It's what I was meant to do, what I was meant to be. I knew that right after my first MMA practice."

— JON JONES

* * *

Art has always been a major part of my life, from doodling on my mom's notepads to late-night painting sessions through the streets of Sacramento to my eventual tenure as a professional artist. It was during that time that I began dreaming of working in the movie industry and on animated films—DreamWorks Studios, to be exact. However, life had another plan. And I had another canvas. Though martial arts not only became my canvas, it also evolved into the driver of my story.

In 2008, I moved into a new condo development. Next door lived a man named Andre Enzensberger. Andre was an independent filmmaker from Germany who was in between projects and looking for his next documentary to film. As time passed, Andre and I ended up becoming friends. We shared art, knocked back some cold ones, and talked about our life stories. Amidst our growing friendship, Andre told me he had not actually seen that many MMA fights, let alone ever met any real fighters. Out of curiosity, he decided to look me up online to see if he could find out more about me. Much to his surprise, there was a ton of information available. In his mind, fighters were supposed to be these big and intimidating tough guys who defied the basic laws of man. Yet, there I was, looking the complete opposite of his preconceived idea. He was blown away and almost couldn't believe his new friend was capable of being one of them.

That moment of awe sparked the idea in him for a new movie. When Andre pitched the documentary to me, it was not originally going to be my story. In fact, it was going to be about his. At the time, Andre's lifestyle was all about partying. And that film idea he had was about an unhealthy filmmaker who meets an MMA fighter that inspires him to change his ways. Once we started shooting, Andre quickly realized there was a much bigger story to tell—that of my truth, the truth about fighters, and a chronicling of my personal battle in chasing a dream.

As the filming process began, I didn't feel uncomfortable or pressured. By that point, I had already done tons of interviews and even a few commercials, so the fear of cameras being in my face never bothered me. Sometimes I would spend the entire day with Andre. From 6 A.M. until 10 P.M., shooting, reshooting, and discussing ideas.

I was completely invested. Once I accepted my role, the process became natural. It may have annoyed others around me, but I fully enjoyed the freedom to be brutally honest in the pursuit of the rawness of the film.

While shooting, many pivotal and life-changing moments

occurred. The fact that these were captured was incredible. I'd transitioned from this scared tough guy to really finding myself as a fighter and—most importantly—a person. Cutting my hair, divorcing my alter ego, walking in on my cheating girlfriend, and then losing the biggest fight of my career. It was all captured.

When the shooting was finally over, we knew we had something very special on our hands. I first watched my story in a private screening room with the director. As the movie played, I was so immersed in how well it was done that I completely forgot it was my story. Every scene was exciting, and I couldn't wait to see what happened next. It was an emotional journey, and the way Andre edited the film was truly amazing. He really brought to life the truth about what it is like to be a fighter in this unforgiving sport. It was something different and surely something inspirational to anyone who watched it. We were convinced that as soon as we started submitting it to festivals, it would win awards and become a widely distributed piece of art. But there was one problem. Festivals were not interested in showing a film about an MMA fighter.

Submissions after submission were responded to with denial letters. We were heartbroken. Eight months of filming, hundreds of hours of footage, countless hours of editing. All dedicated to this project. We really felt it was a story that everyone could relate to. Yet, not a single event was willing to screen our film. In Andre's eyes, it was still an absolute masterpiece. Our prize was who we both became as a result of the process.

Eventually, we accepted our fate and just about gave up. It was then that a friend mentioned a start-up distribution company to Andre. According to him, they desperately need content for their library. We figured it couldn't hurt to send them the film. After all, any viewership would be better than what we were getting. Little did we know that would be the moment when everything changed.

So, we submitted the film with really low expectations of any response. Man, we were wrong! They not only loved it, they wanted to fully back the project and lock in a complete distribution deal with us. That meant the film would be released on iTunes, Netflix, On Demand, all major gaming systems, and even DVD through Amazon. We couldn't believe it. It was like a dream come true. The film was released and quickly became one of the hottest documentaries on iTunes. *Occupation Fighter*, at one point, was rated the number one sports documentary. Then it broke the top ten overall for sports films.

We were even ranked higher than the iconic film *Happy Gilmore*. Talk about a successful release! When Netflix picked it up, we were one of the only MMA films to be on their platform. It was incredibly surreal for us. We then started getting fan emails and letters from people worldwide, thanking us for my story.

Shortly after, Netflix launched another documentary about an upcoming fighter named Dustin Poirier, who later went on to the UFC and became Lightweight World Champion. So, it was safe to say we were among good company on the streaming platform! When our one-year contract with Netflix was set to expire, we became one of the first documentaries to get resigned for another year of distribution. This later led to us landing TV deals with the U.K., Brazil, and eventually into Sports Illustrated digital content. The success of the film outgrew any of our expectations.

IT'S AMAZING HOW THINGS TURN OUT

When I look back at my life, I see a different person from who I am right now. The point is we change and evolve. As do the situations we find ourselves in. If either Andre or I had stopped believing in our project, if we had simply decided to put it on the shelf, we would have never been able to enjoy the success our film finally gained. Life has taught me a great deal of lessons over these years, but the most important was to never stop believing in yourself and what you create.

With the success of the film, we built a fairly large following of supporters, from athletes to artists, casual fans, and your average person. People loved it. During the film, we highlighted my artwork by hosting a gallery art show in Beverly Hills. At the exhibit, another UFC fighter and I showed off our softer passions. In the film, my softer side was a pivotal element of the storyline that highlights a different face of a fighter. One that most people would never expect. I believe showing this side of combat athletes helps break down the one-dimensional, harmful stereotypes that exist. The event itself was a blast. We had art collectors, friends, and fans from all over attend, along with tons of fighters who dropped in to show their support. *Fight Magazine* dubbed the show as one that was "showing the art in martial arts." This scene ended up getting more attention than we expected. A student of mine, who happened to be an artist for DreamWorks Animation, told me about a crazy idea that he had. At first, he said that the studio holds monthly screenings of films as they are released.

Initially, I didn't know what he was getting at. Then it clicked. There was a possible opportunity to get Occupation Fighter onto that screening schedule. Suddenly, I was back in my childhood. Drawing on a piece of paper, desperately wishing one day to work with DreamWorks Studios, and here I was. On the cusp of just that. Somehow manifesting my film onto the screen at their studio. I was speechless. Not long after, it happened. Occupation Fighter was the focused screening film at the world-famous DreamWorks studios.

We arrived at the lot, and I was in a dream state. This was the team I had always wanted to work for. Now there I was—a fighter, sharing his story in front of an audience of artists and directors responsible for some of the greatest animated films in the history of cinema. During the Q/A, I shared this story and almost came to tears.

I still get messages from people who were inspired by the film because of the connection they felt to my struggles and failures. We all go through various painful periods of self-discovery. It comes complete with ups and downs, but that's what makes us human. Each version of us must face what's next in store. We all are fighting for what we want in life. Many times, things won't go our way, but as long as we keep pushing, as long as we keep fighting. The path will open.

13

HE'S OUT

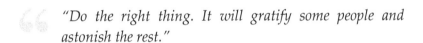 *"Do the right thing. It will gratify some people and astonish the rest."*

— **MARK TWAIN**

I don't remember a single time in my life when I was free of worries. Everything has been a battle. Each moment has been instrumental in building who I am today. If you had asked me, back at the beginning of all this, if I thought any of what I am doing now was possible... I would have told you that you were out of your goddamn mind! But here I am—scarred, callused, still pushing forward. I have always found a way.

A year had passed since my last fight. During that time, I had obsessively worked on my mental and physical health to become stronger than ever. I would say that the traumatic failures of my past no longer haunted me. Instead, they became motivated. My mind was constantly starving for more challenges to overcome. It was time for me to get back into the cage.

I had fought nearly twenty-two fights in my career, but this would be the first event where I would step in confident and completely unfazed by the pressure. My mind had been honed into a weapon—one forged in a fire fueled by the culmination of everything I had been through. This was a new me.

Finally, the fight day arrived, and my opponent looked just like the rising star that was Conor McGregor. Confident, cocky, wanting to rip my head off. At the weigh-ins, he attempted to stare me down. I was unfazed. Instead, I firmly shook his hand and said, "see you tomorrow."

When the main event came, I stood strong in front of a sold-out crowd. Energy radiated from the audience. My opponent paced back and forth, his chest wide open, waiting to smash my head in. As soon as the referee sounded the bell, he rushed toward me. I blast double-legged him to the ground. I took his back and unleashed strikes until he gave me his neck. The fight was over in ninety seconds.

When my hand was raised, I didn't even celebrate. I didn't scream. I didn't dance. Instead, I simply nodded my head and smiled. But it was not arrogance. It was business. I had so much more to do.

THE TRANSITION

For the past seven to eight years, I had run a gym called *PKG* (Punch Kick Grapple). Deep down, I had always known that at some point, I would break off and open my own academy. As an entrepreneur, building someone else's dream is not ideal. And as an athlete, you never know when your competitive days are going to be over. I needed to start planning for my future.

When the idea of opening my own gym sparked, there was a wildfire in my mind that wouldn't let me stop thinking about it. I had been saving most of my fight money over the years, and with that little stockpile of cash, it was time to take the jump.

Daily, I started looking for locations. I began pricing mats and equipment while building imaginary classes in my mind. Then reality hit me. *Holy shit. Opening a facility is expensive.* I couldn't afford anything that I was looking at. The dream quickly returned to being only a dream.

A few months passed, and I still had not seen any progress. Then, something unexpected happened. A good friend of mine —Daniel Collins—told me about a warehouse space that he managed. In fact, he also trained in it. Danny was a purple belt in Jiu-Jitsu and had a few fights under his belt. When he told me where it was located, I absolutely did not want to be on that side of town. It was smack in the middle of a rough neighborhood, just next to Compton and Inglewood... both of which I am sure you are familiar with from music and movies. Initially, I didn't even give it any real thought and just dismissed it. That was until I checked it out.

Hidden in a business park alley of Gardena was this beat-up-looking warehouse. It had high vaulted ceilings, a few bathrooms, and a large open space. Danny already had mats in the facility for his own training. The place needed a lot of work, but something felt special about it. I had never even considered being this far out from the west side of LA. But, if one thing I have learned remains true, opportunity can take you anywhere.

When I arrived, I took some photos of the entire area and showed them to a few friends. The feedback was not positive. They all told me it was not a good place to consider and that it'd cost me more money than it was worth. Yet, a voice inside me kept telling me otherwise. With my background in graphic design, I did the best thing I could think of—I digitally mocked up the entire place, as I envisioned what it might look like.

After seeing what was possible, the excitement of it being a reality took over. My blood boiled. I could not sleep at night. I knew it was the place. I had to make it happen. After presenting the new visual renders to my friends—who'd initially laughed at the dump of a location—even they were convinced. Realizing this was going to happen, my next obstacle was the process of leaving my current gym.

I knew it was not going to be easy. In fact, it was one of the hardest decisions I have ever made. It felt like a bad breakup. I had built close relationships with the members, the fighters, and the community. The idea of departing made me feel sick to my stomach.

And then there was still so much uncertainty. I had no guarantee that I would succeed. There'd be no more consistent paychecks. I was going to walk into this world of the unknown with nothing but the hope that I'd make it through. This whole process seemed eerily similar to when I first decided to fight. I knew I had to make it happen. I couldn't let the fear of failing win. Everything I have been through helped me maintain faith while pushing forward. Just like when I committed to fighting, I went all in. I zeroed out my bank account, quit my job, and put it all into building the gym.

Paint, mats, graphics, construction, apparel—I spent the next five months creating the academy I had always wanted. It became the perfect chance for me to combine my artistic background and my fight experience. The next task was to finalize the logo and name. There were hundreds of ideas floating around, but I needed something iconic and, at the same time, simple.

Then, all of a sudden, it clicked. That's it, *California Mixed Martial Arts.* Clean and direct. After that, the designing of the logo also became easy. Red, white, blue, and a bear. I must have designed hundreds of variations until I found one that spoke to my soul. The next challenge, the biggest challenge, was to get people in the door.

Initially, that wasn't easy. Sure, I had a few fighters and students come with me from the old gym, which helped cover the basic bills, but the facility remained mostly empty over those initial months. I was completely broke, with no idea how I was going to make it work. Concerns began clouding and then penetrating my mind.

I was constantly thinking things like,

Why would people pay to train with me?

How many students do I need to sign up just to break even?

How long will it be before I make any money?

All real worries. All feeding off each other. I could see myself falling deeper into that negative cycle with each passing day.

I needed to create some hype and momentum.

As my next fight approached—which was a big one—I started recruiting athletes to the gym so they could help me train. This was for Bellator MMA, the largest promotion in the world next to the UFC. I used the preparation for that fight to help me market the gym. As training went on, more athletes began showing up for their own camps. People started talking about my gym, and classes began to expand. One student became three, three became ten, and we slowly started filling up. It was amazing, but it meant I needed help. I originally only had three classes per week, which was no longer enough to meet demand. It meant bringing on other fighters to start teaching, just like I did when I first started. Funny how it all comes full circle! And that's how the academy was able to begin offering a full schedule of classes six days a week.

Now, as well as being faced with a huge extra workload, I needed to figure out how to not only run the school but also develop curriculums for teaching. This was a real struggle. I had no clue how to do any of it. Everything needed to be done and fast. There was no time to waste. It was just like a fight. I had to find a way.

Through tons of trial and error, I slowly started creating not just a fight gym but a proper martial arts academy that was a manifestation of the dream I have cherished for so many years. Everything was coming together.

I remember hoping that my debut with Bellator would continue that momentum.

HE'S OUT

When you're tired, when things are no longer fun, that is when your truth is exposed. In fighting, things stop being fun very quickly. We have to make decisions in the heat of the moment. Sometimes they are right, and sometimes they are not. Some will make you, and others will break you. I have experienced both. When I made my debut for Bellator, I had no idea that a decision I was going to make would create worldwide headlines and have some of the biggest names in combat sports talking about it.

In the first round, I shot in for a takedown. My opponent, Mark Vorgeas (a blackbelt in Jiu-Jitsu), grabbed my neck in an attempt to secure a guillotine choke. It was something we had planned for and practiced counters to in the locker room. I started by placing my arm over his shoulder to stop the pressure of the choke while my other arm trapped his hands.

This defense is one that I use all the time in the gym but is rare to see in competition. It's known as a Von Flue choke. By holding the position, your opponent cannot release his own grips, and your shoulder is secured to his neck, creating a nasty blood choke.

The referee had no idea that I was applying my own submission. I could feel Mark's breathing getting heavy. Then, for a second, his body went limp.

The fight was over. I released and moved my head to make sure I had made the right decision. I pointed out to the referee that my opponent was unconscious. He didn't believe me because of the type of choke.

As I postured up and yelled, "He's out!"

The referee replied, "No, he's not. Keep fighting."

I had to make a real decision. Do I punish the helpless man under me, or do I take the risk and walk away? I chose to walk away. The referee then stood over my opponent and realized that he, in fact, was indeed out and then eventually waived the fight off.

At that moment, I did what seemed right to me. Shit, I can only hope someone might have the same compassion if the roles were reversed. We are martial artists. Not animals. When the fight is over, it's over. He has a family to go home to. Walking away from a fight without being severely injured is my goal, and I want the same for my opponents.

Twenty-four hours hadn't even gone by, and the media was going crazy. The video of the walk-away argument with the referee was all over the news. Millions of views and shares. Unbelievable outreach from all around the world. Mike Tyson tweeted about it, Fedor Emelienko, TMZ, Reddit, and even World Star Hip Hop had a thread about it. It was everywhere. That fight was in 2015. Since then, the submission has been called one of the greatest sportsmanship moments in combat sports history. But for me, I was just doing what I thought was right. It could have very easily gone in another direction and been an ugly repeat of what happened in the WEC against Antonio Bañuelos when I thought he tapped.

After the fight was over and the magnitude of the exposure set in, that was a perfect time to re-pitch me to get back in the UFC. Sadly, they did not see it the same way. The UFC brass complimented me on my nobility, but they wanted killers. They wanted brutal fighters that needed to be dragged off their opponents.

That left me broken, with my heart in shambles. I had made so much growth in my personal development that the desire to inflict more damage than necessary to win a fight was just not in me. I couldn't do it. And why was that a bad thing? It was time to make some real decisions. Was this sport even still for me? I couldn't answer that. For the first time in 10 years, I had lost the fire and was no longer certain about wanting to continue.

In a sport that needs one hundred percent commitment, I again was left with no guarantees. So, I announced my retirement from MMA.

14

FINDING YOUR LANGUAGE

> *"Our language is the reflection of ourselves. A language is an exact reflection of the character and growth of its speakers."*

— CESAR CHAVEZ

* * *

When I stepped away from fighting in the cage, I still needed to figure out what came next. The competition had always been what drove me, but what happens when that's gone? That is a world-shattering question that most athletes never get guidance with. Myself included. Instead of planning for the future and putting away money while they are still competing, athletes often fail to save money. Then they stop being able to compete. And when that happens, they'll be able to sustain themselves on their past glory... but only for so long. Until it doesn't. Then many fall victim to a deep depression after finding themselves barreling down dark paths that wind up tearing down their mental and physical health. Watching reruns of old fights while drinking warm beer at 2 P.M. and lamenting about 'the good old days' isn't what I wanted for myself.

Luckily for me, the curse of my ADHD (attention deficit hyperactivity disorder) never lets me settle. I have always had to find my next thing and chase it. Part of me always knew what it was. I just never listened.

There's a saying that reads, "the mats never lie." When I first started training, it was Jiu-Jitsu that grabbed me. It taught me life lessons without me even knowing. All these years, I've credited fighting as what defined me. It wasn't. At least, not specifically. It was Jiu-Jitsu. Day in and day out, it peeled my ego off. It built calluses on not only my body but my mind. It's the only sport in the world that teaches you it's ok to lose.

You (tap) shake your partner's hand and say, "Let's go again."

Each time you do it, you are learning and building. Those lessons are so much more valuable than we realize. And I wanted more of them.

For those who don't know, Jiu-Jitsu is a predominantly ground-based martial art that uses the principles of leverage, timing, and pressure. Also, it requires a decent understanding of human anatomy. Unlike other martial arts—that focus on kicks and punches—Jiu-Jitsu is more about close-contact grappling holds, breaks, and the application of chokes.

Back when professional Jiu-Jitsu was just getting started, a show called *Metamoris* was becoming the UFC of GI and nogi grappling. Up until then, most Jiu-Jitsu tournaments consisted of bracketed competitors, mats on a gymnasium floor, and multiple simultaneous matches. Not this one. Metamoris had a single, white elevated mat in the middle of an arena. Just big enough for two competitors at a time. This format became the blueprint for the modern 'super fights' that showcase today's world-class grapplers.

Once the show started, each athlete was introduced with entrance music as they made their way to the stage like in any other combat sport. But here's the difference—unlike all other Jiu-Jitsu competitions that you pay to compete in, this one paid you. Because of that, everyone wanted to be there. Including me.

It was the spark I needed. I would watch these elite grapplers and know, on a deep level, that I belonged among them. Just as I did back when I watched the WEC. I had a new competitive fire. For two years, I competed almost every month. During that time, I started making a name for myself in the Jiu-Jitsu community. In fact, it was so much that other fighters started coming to me for their training. Even my close friend and top UFC bantamweight, Pedro Munhoz, used to referee a lot of my matches. Today, I have traveled the world training and coaching with him for his fights in the UFC.

Eventually, my shot came. I was a brown belt at the time, and Metamoris typically only allowed black belts to fight on their stage. But, given my MMA credentials and the titles I had been acquiring on the mats, they offered me a spot on a new event called *Metamoris Challengers*. It was a super fight tournament for up-and-coming names to compete in a winner takes all cash prize event. I had four matches, and I submitted them all with front chokes. This later became the foundation for the development of my headlock strangle system.

Shortly after, athletes from all over were coming to train with me. As a result, the academy started to grow, and my Jiu-Jitsu program began winning championship titles against some of the biggest schools in the sport. Slowly, our name started getting recognized. It was nothing short of amazing. The more I coached, the more it became clear. This was my calling. Coaching had given me a platform and a voice to help others achieve greatness and overcome all the bullshit that they were wading through. At the core of it resides one guiding truth—If I can do it, so can you.

TOUGH LOVE

I had been training with my professor for 12 years. He used to smash me into the ground. Many times, I would tap just to his pressure. In the beginning, I used to think he was just a dick. It wasn't until later that I realized how important those lessons were. He had forced me to remove my ego from the equation. I remember a time when I desperately wanted to know what he would like to see from me in order to work toward receiving my blackbelt. Now—and if you know anything about Jiu-Jitsu, you already know this—that was a big no-no. You DO NOT ask when you are getting promoted. I thought I was strategic and stealthy with my questioning.

"Professor Sean," I asked, "Just curious, what are you looking for from me as a blackbelt?"

His response is one I will never forget.

"I don't know, never really thought about it."

My heart sunk. That was not what I'd expected, not at all.

It wasn't until a year later that I finally got my blackbelt. But it wasn't ever about the accolades or trophies. It was about my growth as a person and the direction of my journey. During the ceremony, Professor Sean mentioned that same conversation. He said that when I asked about getting promoted, he really had not put much thought into it. Just the simple fact of me bringing it up meant that I wasn't ready. And he was right. It was one of the biggest lessons I have ever learned. Jiu-Jitsu is not just conducted on the mats but in every aspect of life.

My next challenge was at EBI (The Eddie Bravo Invitational) —an event that was for the elite nogi grapplers, which sparked the explosion of leg lock attacks in combat sports. Most notably, it produced the champion Eddie Cummings who arguably was the best leg locker in the world.

As expected, I was an underdog in the 16-man tournament. Every spot in the bracket was filled by black belts with long lists of accomplishments. My first match was against one of the most experienced competitors in the event. I believe it was his seventh EBI entry. But his tenure didn't bother me. I would go on to beat him in overtime. Next up would be the man everyone was there to challenge, the boogieman himself, Eddie Cummings. I wasn't afraid. I'd intensely studied leg locks and was genuinely excited to test myself. He was my chance. I mean, c'mon! I'm used to getting punched in the face! Thirty-seven seconds later, it was over. Eddie caught me with one of the slickest heel hooks I had ever seen. I had no clue how it happened. There are levels to this game. I needed to start studying more. Much more.

Professor Sean and I began dissecting what happened. We first focused on the positions, then the grips and mechanics. Then came intensive tape study of his teammates and coaches. It was then that we noticed something big. They all had a system behind how they attacked, like a language that only they knew. It was as if we were decoding a puzzle. I started applying this concept of language to all my attacks. Legs, chokes, and even my overall approach to the matches changed. I didn't care about what you were good at. I just had to not let you win an argument with me in an area where you might be more fluent. After arming myself with all that new data, I had to test it.

My next match would have me travel across the country to New Jersey to face Frank Rosenthal in a main event super fight. Frank was a teammate and student of Eddie Cummings. It was time to put my new data to the test. My goal? Simple—dive into the fire of his leg game and prove that I speak that language. And I did. For 10 minutes, we attacked each other from the ground, both nearly securing finishes. Though I ended up losing in overtime, I didn't care. I'd proved to myself the concept of language works. My goal was reached.

One of the biggest lessons I have learned over all these years of fighting is that everything we do is data. So, collect as much knowledge as possible and then push yourself to test that information. I guess you could say I have developed an obsession with it. My next challenge was going to be at the IBJJF Nogi Worlds. In previous years, I had already won titles from blue belt through brown. But it was different this time. It would be my first world tournament at the blackbelt level. My confidence was at an all-time high, and it showed. I submitted my first two opponents, then won the semifinal match by points. That left me to face the seven-time world champion, Samuel Braga. He was a legend.

Throughout the tournament, nobody even came close to scoring on him. But I did. Imagine how a new blackbelt would feel when facing off against one of the greatest. That was the challenge I wanted. As soon as the match began, I shot a fast double to try and score. His butt hit the floor, but—for what I can only guess were political reasons—no points were given for the takedown. The match continued as we scrambled back and forth. I secured my now infamous D'arce choke. He escaped, but that would put me up on the scorecard.

The clock ran down, and the referee began warning me for stalling. I continued to try and pass the guard while attempting not to get swept. The referee again called me for stalling— putting a negative point against me, and putting him in the lead with only thirty seconds left on the clock. Seeing the time, Braga held on just enough to make sure that he secured the win. Inches away from dethroning the world champion, I would take the silver medal and stand in second place. Maybe I was robbed, maybe not. Either way, I came closer to beating him than anyone else in the past seven years. In my first year as a blackbelt.

Now knowing that I could compete against the elite grapplers of the sport, it was clear that my time was coming. I just needed to keep collecting more data and keep building my language of Jiu-Jitsu.

15

BIRTH OF COMBAT JIU-JITSU

 "The will to win, the desire to succeed, the urge to reach your full potential... these are the keys that will unlock the door to personal excellence."

— CONFUCIUS

* * *

One day a student came to me with a personal plea for help. Never having spoken to anyone about it before, he asked to sit down and talk about what was going on in his life. Major challenges. He had a fight coming up, his first in over three years. With a record of 0-3, the fears of him failing again plagued him, and he was coming up with every reason as to why he shouldn't fight... problems at home and at work, not having enough time for training, etc. He then told me how he hadn't been staying focused during all of his previous fights. He was also looking for reasons he shouldn't train and avoid repeating his previous failures. This would have been our first fight together.

I asked him a few questions about his fears and uncovered that one of them was him being afraid to fail in front of me. Now, this type of mindset is very common… and if you've read this far, then you know I'm no exception! We put these ideas in our heads—we coach ourselves on why were aren't good enough or how we might let someone else down. But let's take a second to get real and honest here. At the end of the day, WHO FUCKING CARES? These are your shoes. And you have to walk home in them.

This is your life. Fuck what anyone else thinks or has to say about it. If you want to accomplish great things, go do it. It's really that idiotically simple! The need to prove ourselves to others is one of the greatest lies we can tell ourselves. And I should know. I did it for most of my life. Where did that get me?

I used to think that I couldn't say I was good at something because I never wanted to come off as cocky or egotistical. The dark side to that thinking was that I would never give myself credit for anything. All my small wins were constantly overshadowed by some kind of negative inner dialogue. As a result, I would expect everything to fall apart when it mattered most. And when it inevitably did, it was easy to place the blame on anything or anyone other than myself. Personal accountability was non-existent. Deep down, I knew what the root problem was.

Our inner dialogue and how we see ourselves is the only thing that truly matters. We all talk to ourselves. Don't try and act like you don't. Every situation that occurs will result in either positive or negative self-talk. In general, society conditions us to look for easy solutions to complex problems. But at the same time, we tend to make complex issues out of simple problems.

It wasn't until I was deep into my fighting career that I

finally understood the reasons why I fought. It was simple. I was terrified. I had been afraid of just about everything. From me being a pussy, to just not being seen as one of the cool kids. Those failures were complete self-sabotaging. My focus was on how other people saw me instead of on the one person whose opinion of me mattered the most. Me.

Once I finally understood that, my obsession with the discovery of the mind took off. Through reading daily and listening to audiobooks in the car (so don't try and tell me you don't have time to read), I gorged myself on as much brain food as possible. The more I learned, the stronger I became. Competing was slowly turning into my own science project for gathering data.

In November 2017, my mind was on a whole new level as I was accepted in the inaugural four-man Combat Jiu-Jitsu (CJJ) tournament. It was a blackbelt, invitational event where open-hand palm strikes on the ground were allowed. This was the first event like it in history and would be seen live on UFC Fight Pass. The familiar nerves of competition flooded my mind, but at the same time, I was excited to test my mettle against some of the best grapplers in the world that were selected to compete within this new rule set.

Days before the event, on what should have been my last hard day of training, stupid luck struck again. While escaping a position, my rib dislocated and popped out of place. Every breath I took was excruciatingly painful. With each inhale, it felt like a weight was being pressed against my chest. My toxic past habit of criticizing and sabotaging thinking came rushing back into my mind.

"Now we don't have to fight anymore."

"Let's go and stuff our faces with junk food."

"Thank God! I won't let anyone down now."

"Everyone will understand."

But something was different. For the first time in my life, I realized that I had complete control over how my mind talks to itself. I was the one creating the thoughts. It was at that moment I made the decision to never again fall victim to my own negativity. It was time to become a champion of the mind. Victory was no longer purely external; it no longer only meant having my hand raised. Victory then became overcoming my own perceived limitations and rising above any bullshit doubt.

I would spend the next few days doing rehab as much as possible. I was not going to pull out. This would have been the first-time making weight at one hundred and thirty-five pounds on the same day as the event. If I could pull that off, then that would be yet another victory. I started making milestones that I celebrated. Every day became something special.

Even something as simple as making my bed after getting up, I considered a victory. This mental exercise eventually brought me back into the zone. I started with a slow jog. Then came sprints. And the sprints finally led me to believe that I could still pull this off.

Fight day soon arrived. I still hadn't trained with anyone since the rib injury. There was no way for me to gauge how I would perform, but I didn't care. My first fight was going to be with the scale.

Victory! I'd hit my target weight. One hundred thirty-five pounds. I'd made it! It was a huge deal for me. I'd had to overcome a major mental battle and prove to myself that I could do something that seemed almost impossible.

A few hours passed, then it was time to warm up. My rib felt surprisingly ok. Not amazing, but good enough to compete. So, I took a deep breath in and felt it pinch with a sharp pain. At the same time, my name was called out to enter the stage.

"Chad, let's go! You're up next!"

It was time to make history.

The fear of failure didn't seem to exist. I was so happy with where my mind was at. The training camp, the injury, making weight, and finally being there and standing tall above any excuses. I was already winning. Whatever happened during the fight was just a bonus.

The crowd was silent as my ten-minute bout against standout grappler JM Holland began. No one knew what to expect. We were the first to ever do this on such a massive platform. My opponent slid right to the ground, allowing me to start striking. I loaded up on a giant left hand and launched it at him. It was a swing-and-miss—the crowd jumped out of their seats in excitement. The entire auditorium erupted, going from a room full of deafening silence to an absolute roar.

After the first strike, it was a full-blown dogfight. Back and forth we went, landing big shots, slaps, and submission attempts. Both of us were looking for any angle to get the finish. During a brief pause in the action, I relaxed for a second. Bad decision. JM latched onto one of my arms and threw his legs over my neck, trapping me in a triangle choke, landing me in big trouble. My only option was to pull out forcefully before getting strangled. When my head escaped the hold, a loud pop filled the air. My rib fully dislocated. I only had two minutes remaining in the fight. With my adrenaline going crazy, I postured up and powered through the pain.

Whatever was going to happen next had nothing to do with the man against me in the fight. It was all about the one inside my head.

I could hear the time being called:

"Ninety seconds left!"

"Sixty seconds left!"

"He's breaking!"

I could see my opponent starting to fade away with every shot I landed. In the last fifty seconds, I secured one of my favorite chokes (ol' faithful D'arce) and forced him to tap. And with that, history was made.

The match was over, but there was no time to celebrate my

victory. We still had one fight in the finals. As I walked off the mat and into the locker room, I collapsed to the floor. The pain from my injured rib was unbearable. I couldn't talk or breathe. Everything hurt.

Suddenly, I began vomiting. The pain stemming from my rib began a vicious cycle. The more I vomited, the more pain I was in. The more pain I was in, the more I vomited.

It was something we needed to keep secret from the athletic commission, or they would have immediately pulled me out of the tournament.

When asked what was wrong, Josh Barnett said it was just dehydration. The truth is, none of us knew how bad it really was. Luckily, my chiropractor—Dave Reed—was with us backstage and attempted to shove the rib back in place as best he could. Everyone thought I was done. Everyone except me. Quitting after coming this far was simply not an option. Then luck seemed to be on my side.

My opponent for the finals had just finished his fight. He was wrecked beyond fatigue. As I watched him lying there, pitifully gasping for air, the show informed us that we might be going up very soon. Everything depended on how long the next two matches in front of ours ran for—perhaps ten minutes, perhaps an hour.

There wasn't any doubt about it. I was in bad shape. However, I jokingly told my team that I could still beat a dead guy. As my mind began to settle in, I acknowledged that no matter what happened, *I am a champion*. This was the proof I had been searching for my entire life.

After fifty minutes had passed, the moment of truth was upon us. Unfortunately for me, because of the long delay, my opponent had fully recovered and no longer appeared to be on his deathbed. He stood across from me, an intense hunger glinting in his eyes, eager to prove himself after what he'd gone through earlier. I was completely unfazed. To me, I had already won. The true battle was being waged in my mind, and I was ready to die on my shield.

Just as the fight started, I felt the side effects from the damaged rib flaring up. With my breathing so shallow, my ability to grab was simply non-existent. He shot in for a takedown and landed directly on my chest. There was nothing I could do to stop it. On the ground, I fought as hard as I could, but the pain was just too much. I couldn't get him off me and ended up losing by submission.

On that night, my hand was not raised in the finals, and yet I walked away more victorious than I could ever have imagined. I had conquered the negative voice in my head. I had made a choice to define for myself what constitutes a true champion.

ADVERSITY CREATES GREATNESS

After the success of the first Combat Jiu-Jitsu event, it became the talk of the community. Everyone wanted to see what was going to happen next.

Eddie Bravo, the vision behind EBI, decided to bring the best grapplers and MMA fighters together to compete for the first-ever CJJ world championship title. This, again, would be featured live on UFC Fight Pass. Myself and seven other elite athletes were selected to compete. It was my chance at redemption. Only now, it would be even tougher. With eight people in the tournament, I would have to win three fights in a single night to be crowned champion.

The crackling fear of the competition excited me. For the six weeks prior, I'd trained like a madman. My diet was pristine. Every morning I would wake up and run three miles before practice. I was not willing to let any shortfall be due to a failure in preparation.

THE WEIGHT CUT

Cutting weight is synonymous with combat sports. Many would even say it's the hardest part. For years, I have been used to extreme dieting and harsh weight drops. In high school, I would jog in plastics, spit in a cup, and only eat ice cubes for a week to get my weight down. Today's ways are a little more humane, but that doesn't mean they are any less dangerous. Unknowingly, I was about to enter the worst cut of my life.

The experience of making weight with a busted rib instilled a confidence in me that I could easily do it again. Wow, was I so wrong! Despite my diet being perfect and following a cutting regimen that was identical, my body just didn't want to listen.

I began my cut from around a hundred and forty-five pounds. Nothing uncommon for me. Using the bathtub, Epsom salt, and a body lathered in Albolene, my weight was coming down with ease. The system I use typically removes up to a pound and a half of water every fifteen minutes. With each passing interval, everything seemed to be going as planned. That was until I hit three pounds away from my target. Oh, hello, extreme pain in my back! The dehydration was affecting my kidneys, which were now cramping. After another fifteen minutes in the bathtub, the pain was so intense that it forced me into the fetal position as I dry heaved from overwhelming nausea. My organs were beginning to fail.

This was an experience that neither my team nor I had ever dealt with. The exact fears everyone has about weight cutting exist for a reason. I couldn't pull myself out of the tub, and nobody knew what to do. The easiest answer was simple, end the punishment. Begin hydrating and withdrew myself from the event. I wasn't ready to do that. I had to keep fighting. We drained the tub and pulled me out.

Unable to stand without pain, I laid on the floor for another twenty minutes, wrapped in towels and with the heater on.

Everyone was beyond worried. This is the stuff people die from. I was running out of time, and the weigh-in cut-off was approaching. My heart told me I wasn't going to make it. I finally got off the ground and stepped onto the scale. It read one hundred thirty-five- and one-half pounds. *Ho-ly shit!* I was on weight. A rush of energy zapped through my body. Like magic, the pain went away. I threw my clothes on and rushed to the official weigh-ins.

I knew from the beginning that if I was going to have any chance at winning this tournament, I would have to battle through many moments of uncertainty. That had just been one of them, and it was just the beginning. As I stood in front of the media, cameras, and opponents, I had to hide the lingering dizziness and pain. I couldn't let anyone see my true state. The official weight was called, and unfortunately, my next challenge was still not even at the event. Time was limited to recover. I only had six hours to hydrate, eat, and rest my body in preparation to fight multiple times in one night. To help the process, a nurse friend came over and gave me an IV filled with fluids and minerals. This is normally something routine. Super straightforward. But for Chad here, as you may have come to expect by now, it was not. I was so dehydrated that the needle was unable to go into a vein. After several attempts and an hour lost, we finally got one in. Two bags of fluid later, I began returning to life. The pain in my back was gone. My cheeks were no longer sunken. And most importantly, I was slowly able to start eating. It was time to face the music and head to the arena.

This tournament was stacked with eight of the best grappling athletes in the world. From blackbelt champions to UFC stars, the competition level was insane. Each match would consist of ten-minute regulation rounds, plus overtime with the fastest escapes or finishes from selected positions.

My first opponent was set to be a grappling legend, Barret Yoshida. Unfortunately, UFC bantamweight Wilson Reis missed weight, and that meant the entire bracket was shuffled around. I would now have to get past the first round before we had our chance to fight.

It was time to start warming up. To my surprise, I felt incredible. The fact that I had been knocking on death's door just hours prior seemed to only spur me on.

The first round got underway, and I won with a D'arce choke in under a minute. The tone for the night was set. Barret lost in the opening fight, and I would now face the man who beat the legend. The old me would have been terrified. But not me on that day. I was on a mission to prove that I was on a different level. Winning this next match would again put me in the finals.

For ten minutes straight, I outwrestled my opponent and eventually submitted him in overtime with a rear-naked choke. As I released the hold, I pointed to the crowd and shook my finger to the sky, saying, "I told you!"

It was clear that there was a fire burning fiercely in me. Uninjured this time, I again made it to the finals. My opponent was Renzo Gracie's blackbelt and MMA veteran Sidmar Honorio. This guy beat the shit out of everyone on his side of the bracket. It felt like a war was coming. On the other side of it, one of us was going to emerge as the first-ever CJJ world champion.

Bruce Buffer called us to the center stage as the entire Florentine Gardens crowd stood to their feet. This felt bigger than any other event I had ever competed in. We shook hands. It was on. Each time we tied up, I would blast a takedown and smash him with strikes as we hit the ground. I didn't want this going into overtime.

As the clock ran down, I secured another takedown. This time, I stood up in the guard and threw his legs to the side while delivering a massive overhand palm strike that bounced his head off of the canvas, almost knocking him out cold. Victory was tantalizingly close. I just needed to stay on the offensive. I just needed to keep at him. And I did. After landing a few more strikes, my opponent managed to roll into a leg lock, almost securing a heel hook as the bell rang. We went overtime.

This was going to come down to who wanted it more. I had already been fighting for over twenty-five minutes between my three matches, and Sidmar was going to have the first pick of position. He chose to start on my back. As the round started, I exploded out of his control in just thirty seconds. Again, I threw my hands up to the crowd in excitement as I rushed back to the mat. I was now only seconds away from becoming champion. Two options for that presented themselves—either hold the position longer than he did or somehow find a submission. I took his back and waited for the ref.

"Three, two, one...GO!"

My opponent strained and struggled with all his energy. I could feel my lock slipping. Instead of trying to hold, I threw a few strikes that raised his chin to the sky. This allowed me to slip my arm across and secure another rear naked choke. He. Fucking. Tapped.

At the age of thirty-six, I'd become the first-ever Combat Jiu-Jitsu world champion. I dropped to my knees in tears, overcome with a cascade of raw emotion. It'd been the performance of a lifetime. But to hell with the external achievement—I'd proven to myself that I belonged with the elite.

Once the tournament was over, it wasn't the belt or title that was the greatest prize. It was the conversation with my dad. Over all the years that I'd been competing, it had never felt like I was able to make him proud. That night was different. Instead of having something negative to say, or really anything at all, he just sat with me and cried tears of unencumbered joy.

16

END OF A JOURNEY

"Life takes on meaning when you become motivated, set goals, and charge after them in an unstoppable manner. You must remain focused on your journey to greatness."

— **LES BROWN**

* * *

The career of a professional athlete usually lasts between five and seven years. I have doubled that. Over the past decade and a half, my body has been thrashed, and it has been broken. Every day I wake up to something new hurting, from the ongoing back issues to herniations in my neck or the endless litany of other annoying injuries. So much has become clear as I get older, namely that my body is not wanting to work for me anymore.

THE COMEBACK KID

It had been almost three years since my last MMA fight. During my time away from the ring, I spent countless hours developing my relationship with Jiu-Jitsu, but I was also tearing my body down further.

I'd always known that, at some point, I would put the gloves back on. I just didn't know when that would be or when I would have the drive to step back into the cage. In 2018 Bellator would call again and present a great opportunity in my hometown—a fight against James Barnes. A Jiu-Jitsu blackbelt, All-American wrestler, and holder of an intimidating record of fourteen and three. He was not an easy opponent! Especially coming off such a long hiatus.

The consequential fear from what we call ring rust entered my mind, but I refused to listen. I had been competing the entire time against the best grapplers in the world. I needed to know two things—had that time spent away been worth it, and was I ready to charge back into a real fight? I got my answer to both of those questions. By the end of the second round, I had battered my opponent from bell to bell, leaving him barely able to get off the canvas. Instead of walking back to my corner, I stood defiantly in the middle of the cage to let him know he still had five more minutes with me. That was enough for his team to throw in the towel. The fight was over and declared a TKO victory.

Winning felt amazing. Unfortunately, that feeling didn't last long. All my injuries over the years reared their heads again, and I began to spiral. In the weeks that followed, I was barely able to walk. My sciatica returned, and I lost the ability to move my neck. I was falling apart.

You could say I have paid the price for success. And in return, I wouldn't say you were wrong. I would say nothing comes for free… though I honestly have no clue how a lost kid from Sacramento turned his life around and ended up making a career out of fighting. If you would have asked me at the beginning where I saw this all going, I sure as hell wouldn't have dreamed up a story like this.

When I started, I was a scared and confused kid that didn't know who he was. I had no confidence and was malleable, aimless, and influenced by my surroundings. Somehow, I continued down a path of trial and error. That somehow led to fighting in a three-story bar in Mexico, to fighting against the best fighters on the planet for the biggest organizations. It has meant squaring up against new versions of myself constantly. It has meant detecting and removing my own bullshit on a daily basis, grinding down my ego, and building up calluses on my skin and mind.

Over the years, I've come to appreciate what differentiates winners from champions and what it means to lead by example. That discovery has not only changed my life, it has given me a voice to connect with anyone who has ever been counted out.

When I opened my gym, it was with a vision of creating an environment for people to sculpt their inner champions. On the mats, in life, and—if they chose—in the ring. I wanted to make an impact on the world by building something I wish I'd had when it all started.

A place that inspired anyone to want to be a champion.

A place that made them believe they could be more than they ever thought possible.

A full-circle support system was the vision.

Changes that I have empowered others to make in themselves are far greater accomplishments than any award or title I have won. Watching people overcome ignites my fire. It reminds me of the importance of what I am doing and why I have sacrificed so much. But yeah, of course, I can't deny that there is a lot more I wish I could have done in my career! Here's the thing though—eventually, I had to be honest with myself.

The injuries I have sustained over the years have caught up with me. By the end, my body just wasn't working the same anymore. Every day I'd walk into the gym looking like the Hunchback of Norte-Dame! Sure, I was still training, but nothing like what was needed if I wanted to keep pursuing competition like I had.

One of the biggest things I teach is that if you set out to accomplish a goal, you do it. The more it scares you, the more you must keep pushing forward. I am living proof of that being possible. Fighting has been such a massive part of my life; you could even say it has defined it. But these days, I reflect daily on how I can impact and empower more people. How can I help sculpt more champions? I knew what the answer was. It was finally time for me to put the same passion into coaching as I did into fighting. It was time to move on.

That decision hit me when I was thirty-seven years old. Thirteen months had passed since my fight in Bellator. My neck was a mess, the sciatica was running wild down my leg, and I was also recovering from a torn meniscus and rotator cuff. I could have easily just walked away (or, well, hobbled), and nobody would have tried to convince me otherwise. But I wasn't ready to just say I was done with words. That wasn't the language I'd been learning, after all. I needed to fight against the monster that lived under the bed one more time, needed to take one last stand before I went out on my shield. It was undeniable that the cards were stacked against me. Good thing that was such familiar ground.

I talked with my team and said, "Let's make this happen!"

We laid out a timeline of fifteen weeks to prepare for what would be my last fight. Those fifteen weeks of training would mark the end of my career, and I wanted to make my last minutes in the cage count—to wholeheartedly pour fifteen years into my last fifteen minutes.

I knew this camp was going to be challenging. I needed to

have tons of rehab on my body, train around injuries, coach my fighters, run my academy, and somehow still manage all my other obligations. Those were the expected obstacles, but additional challenges piled up as the weeks went on.

While initially discussing event venues, we spoke with a few big promotions that really wanted me on their show. But traveling for my last fight did not seem like it made sense. I wanted to fight on my home turf in LA. I wanted to be with my crowd, my family, and the city where I'd built my career. So, I spoke with a good friend of mine—one of the top promoters in California, George Bastmajyan—who runs an event called *Light Out Promotions* (LXF). We both got excited after a long talk. It was time to rock and roll. We were going to put together a show Los Angeles would not forget. That is, if my body could hold up and make it to the fight.

As training camp began, I needed to spend the first few weeks doing mostly rehab and therapy. At the same time, the promotion started looking for an opponent. Three weeks in, I was not only feeling better but was also given the name of the fighter who would be my final opponent.

Two weeks later, the promoter called with news that no fighter wants to hear. My opponent had backed out. Luckily, we were still ten weeks away from the event, so we had plenty of time to find a replacement. I remained optimistic and focused. However, adversity has two fists. He would hit again.

During a live wrestling session, my shoulder smashed into the ground, tearing the labrum near my collarbone. I couldn't lift my arm. While I knew going into this fight that previous injuries were going to take a toll, I hadn't banked on sustaining any new ones.

Panic and fear loomed over me, threatening to set in, and the old me probably would have let them. But instead, I refused to be a victim. I put my arm in a sling and finished coaching practice for my athletes.

Over the days that followed, I went back to therapy and continued to work around the new injury. Though I was putting on a brave face, I needed some positive news. Then it came—a new opponent. With less than six weeks left until the fight, it was great to get a name.

Momentarily, my excitement was back. We began researching the fighter. Then, just as quickly as he was in, he was out. Another call came in, but the guy wouldn't sign the contract. Frustrations mounted as I once again had no opponent. So much of me just wanted to call it and say it just wasn't meant to happen.

The fear of the fight not materializing was growing day by day. To add illness to injury, I also came down with a nasty cold. A whole week passed. Then two.

It finally subsided, and I continued to train as if I was the opponent in the mirror. Everything felt like it was going full circle, back to when I stepped into the ring for the very first time back in Mexico. I had no idea who I was fighting, what to expect, or what I was doing. *But I'm here*, I thought to myself. *I am facing the fear yet again.*

With just three weeks to go, the promotion found another opponent. A champion kickboxer. While not the most experienced in MMA, he was a tough and undeniably dangerous fighter from one of Mexico's best gyms. We accepted, and my final countdown began.

For almost every fighter, the last leg of training camp is always the toughest. Dieting kicks into overdrive, and mental focus on the task at hand becomes all-encompassing... so no surprise that this is usually the stage where relationships are tested.

For the past year, I'd given the dating game another try. In fact, I'd met someone on one of those horrific apps. She had never watched a fight, let alone attended one, so hey, I thought, *what a great idea for our first date!* I took her to an event where I was coaching a few of my students. Maybe not the most romantic, sure, but it was a perfect primer for what she was getting herself into.

Fast forward twelve months, and there we are together, preparing for my final bout. Monica was amazing in the kitchen. She handled all my meal prepping, cooking, water loading, and —most of all—my bitching! She made the process simple and easy by taking away all the things I typically have to worry about. Even on the nights that my sciatica flare-ups were so bad that I couldn't stand, she was right there to pick me up off the floor and guide me across the room into bed. For someone that was new to this, she handled it like a battle-hardened veteran. Monica was quickly proving herself to be something more than just a girl I was dating.

FINAL TALK WITH THE TEAM

To wrap up every practice, my team and I would sit down and have a discussion. If guys were scheduled to fight, we'd have them talk about their mindset and how the camp had been for them. After what had seemed like an eternity, my fight was finally one week away. I thanked all my athletes for their motivation and for allowing me to live the dream one last time.

I was honored to share the battle room with each and every one of them. It's so easy to forget how even though only one person goes in and fights, it takes an army to get them there. We all stand on the front lines together. When one of us goes to war, we all march.

The team all stood up as we put our hands in the center of the group,

I call it out:

"War on three"

"One, Two, Three!"

The entire room erupts in unison, shouting, *"WAR!."*

We were all dialed in—an army with a singular goal in mind. Battle was on the horizon.

It was time for the weight cut... the only part of fighting I will honestly not miss. We started at my typical one hundred and forty-six pounds, with twenty-four hours to drop down before the official weigh-in. Six Epsom salt baths later, I was already on target and almost seven pounds down, putting me ahead of schedule. This allowed me to eat an egg and have a little green juice and water before going to bed.

The next morning, I was back up to one hundred and forty-one pounds. Fairly well hydrated and with a bit of food already in my system, I repeated the same water depletion process. Within an hour, I was already on target. This was the easiest my weight had ever come off. Sure, my body felt like shit—and I probably looked like an extra on the walking dead—but none of that mattered. The hard part was over. I had finished my final cut.

We headed to weigh-ins, and all I could think about was the journey I'd been on. Food didn't even cross my mind. All the years of soaring highs and crushing lows came vividly flooding back to me. In the blink of an eye, there I was, standing on the official scale and squaring off with my opponent. There was a crackling intensity between us, and it was clear he was here to win just as much as I was.

All the preparation festivities were now in the past. The only thing left to do was hydrate, refuel, rest, and get ready for war the next day.

Pre-fight nerves hit everyone differently. For me, It has always been hardest once the weigh-ins are done. Reality sets in then, and the torturous waiting game begins. But not that time. Everything seemed brighter and more memorable. From the first meal, to basic fluid intake. Each moment was luminescent. It was a day that had been years in the making, and it did not disappoint.

I booked a room at the venue's hotel (The Burbank Marriott). That night, Monica and I sat by the outdoor fire pit and just relaxed, enjoying each other's company. The stress of fighting wasn't even present. I had been so busy for months that I'd never fully realized how truly special that girl was until then as I looked over at her in the firelight.

It's amazing how someone who knew nothing of this process was able to jump in and stand knee-deep in the trenches with me like that. Having her there allowed me to sleep like a baby, though I couldn't wait for dawn to break and to get down to business.

FIGHT DAY

Everyone handles fight day a little differently. For me, I like to wake up, have my coffee, and get a shakeout in before I eat. A shakeout is a short 30-minute workout that helps get the body moving after a weight cut, and most times, this is done either outside or in a hotel room. Luckily for me, the cage I'd be fighting in was already set up in the hotel's event center. After speaking with the promoters, my coaches and I got a chance to train inside the actual cage before the fight later that evening. One of the workers informed me of a crazy coincidence as I was finishing my workout. Apparently, the canvas inside the cage was the very same one I'd fought on back in Mexico all those years ago. Whether it was true or not, I don't know. But what I do know is that it made me smile and reflect on the incredible journey I was on.

I headed back to my room, ate breakfast, gathered my gear, and took a rest before it was time to check in for the actual event. When I walked down to the arena, my team walked with me. Everyone was decked out in Team Savage warmups. It looked like an army was coming to invade. I shook hands with fans, promoters, and other fighters that I'd known for many years. The sense of community was incredible.

In the locker room, it was time to check my mind in. I laid my fight clothes out, got dressed, and Josh Barnett wrapped my hands. We began the warmup. First was boxing with my coach, Jose, aka "Baby Jesus," then grappling with Victor Henry. My date with destiny was getting closer with every punch I threw.

Knowing that this would be my last time walking into the cage, I wanted to pay homage to my early days and those that'd helped me. But I also wanted to tie it all together somehow and dovetail it with the legacy I wished to leave. No MC rapping, no guys crawling to the cage. None of the ego-driven antics. I wanted to have my younger students walk me in—a symbolic passing of the torch from one warrior to the next generation.

THE LOCKER ROOM

Fighting is a mental battle. It doesn't matter where on a lineup you stand. But when you are the main event, you inevitably have to contend with extra stress and anxiety. You see fighter after fighter coming back to the locker room—some happy, some sad, and some badly bloodied. You need to ignore it all. You must keep your emotions calm. As the night goes on, the room seems to get smaller. All the other fighters are gone until it's just you and your coaches.

That was how it was when the promoters walked in, *"You go out in five minutes, Chad!"*

The kids were escorted in and sat on the floor. I paced the locker room and tried to get my mind right. You could cut the tension in the air... but you'd need a damn sharp knife. One of the kids raised their hand to ask a question. Of course, I let him.

"Why do you walk like an old man?" he asked.

The entire room broke out in laughter. It put a smile on my face, and I gave him a high five for the well-timed humor. That comic relief was exactly what I needed right as the moment had arrived. I took a deep breath and said to myself, *everything is a choice. It's time to be a champion, young man.*

My music started, and the final walk began. Electricity filled the arena as I entered to Queen's "We Will Rock You." The crowd chanted and banged along to the iconic song as my young students, all wearing the academy kimonos, formed a line down the length of the tunnel. I fist-bumped each of their hands on my way to the cage. Standing there in front of Josh, I bit down on my mouthpiece while he gave me two big slaps across the face.

I looked him in the eyes and barked, *"Let's fucking go!"*

Standing in front of the cage door, I almost didn't want to go in. After fifteen years, walking through it was going to be the last time I'd do so as a competitor. I grabbed the top bar and just swung back and forth for a bit. Time seemed to slow down. I let go. I stepped inside. Once my feet touched the canvas, it was time to check in. Fifteen minutes for glory.

As soon as the fight started, I wanted to get right after him. I threw a head kick and slipped on the first attack. It landed me on my back, and my opponent wasted no time jumping on top of me. I rolled into a leg lock and thought it was going to be over then and there. Turning his heel in the opposite direction, I could feel it pop. This kid was tough. Instead of tapping out, he chose to punch me in the face while escaping. I was losing leverage and needed to think quick.

Right as he was about to escape, I slipped out from his legs and ended up on top. Grabbing his neck, I secured a D'arce choke. I squeezed and squeezed, but again he refused to tap. The round ended. Frustration was setting in as I sat down in my corner.

"Why couldn't I finish this guy?" I asked Josh. *"What was I doing wrong?"*

He responded with the simplest advice. *"Nothing, do it again."*

The second round started. I ignored the fatigue in my arms and took Josh's advice by throwing myself right at him again. A flurry of strikes was exchanged. I received a kick to the body that knocked the wind out of me. Instead of gasping for air, I bit down on my mouthpiece and pressed forward. My cross hook landed, followed by an uppercut which smashed him to the canvas.

I jumped on top of him and continued raining down strikes. He reached up to defend himself, giving me a perfect opening for another choke. It was a modified head and arm triangle. I latched on and unleashed pressure that had been 15 years in the making. I didn't know what to expect. This guy was tough. Then it happened. He tapped.

The crowd went wild. But not me. I stayed right there, sitting on the canvas, then hugged my opponent and thanked him for the battle. It was all over. A million emotions rushed over and through me. The most powerful was an overwhelming sense of gratitude for the sport that had given me such an incredible journey. All the years of ups and downs, the struggles and successes. It had all been leading up to that moment. I eventually climbed up on the cage and looked across the crowd.

"Thank you," I uttered as I scanned the sea of faces for my family and girlfriend.

The announcer brought us to the center of the cage and raised my hand. On the mic, I said a few final words:

"In life, we are all fighting for something. I am living proof that if you keep pushing and keep fighting, anything and everything is possible."

The fight was over, but there was still one last thing I had to do. I took my gloves off—carefully placing them in the center of the cage—then kneeled and bowed over them. When I stood up, the gloves remained down to symbolize the final chapter of my journey had come to a close.

That fire, the one that burns for the thrill of competing, is still very much raging within me. To be honest, I don't think it will ever be fully extinguished. Day in and day out, the idea of fighting consumes me. But now I understand what that actually means. I know the mountains that I had to climb and the many more I'm sure are still to be summited. All the heartaches, the hard work, the obstacles, I feel like it was all just yesterday. You can hear it in my passion when I speak to my athletes, in my videos, or anytime I get a chance to talk about the mind. I remain fiercely driven by my journey and by the monster that has tried to chase me my entire life. Whereas fear of failure once held me back, now it is the driving force that propels me forward.

Today, I stand as a testament to the unshakeable truth that anything IS possible. My story is one that many would have said to be impossible—myself included—but here I am. I am nobody special, just a kid that refused to quit when the cards were stacked against him. The fight has always been inside me. It is what connects us all as we go toe to toe with doubts, fears, and people who say we can't do it. But the simple truth is this— being a champion is a choice.

* * *

I hope my story inspires you to see that there resides a champion in all of us. The desire to win. The drive to fight for more. Inevitably, things will get ugly. You're definitely going to get hurt, and you're undeniably going to feel at times like everything is lost. But that is where the magic is made. Being a champion is not about being the strongest. It's not about the biggest or even the best. Being a champion is a mindset. No matter how badly the odds are stacked against you, there is always a way. Life is a journey, and every obstacle is just a chapter of a book that is still being written. This is my story. We all have one. Hopefully, this has opened your eyes to see that you are not alone, that our stories, in many ways, are the same, and that we must fight for everything in life.

As I say to my athletes:

How badly do you want it?

How far are you willing to go?

Are you ready to be a champion?

MAKE A CHOICE.

DUES PAID (INJURY COLLECTION)

As promised, here it is. My list of injuries sustained as a professional athlete. They are the dues I have paid through the years. Your WHY must be stronger than your WHY NOT.

- Scoliosis (Not from fighting, but an obstacle throughout my entire life)
- 12 mm disc herniation in L5 / S1
- Sciatica with nerve damage
- Stenosis in the spine
- Back surgery (Microdiscectomy)
- Bulging disc in the neck (uncertain size)
- Torn labrum in the shoulder
- Torn (groin) adductor on both sides
- Torn rotator cuff
- Torn ac joint in the shoulder
- Torn meniscus on both knees
- Hairline fracture of the femur
- Dislocated rib
- 4 Broken fingers

- 2 Broken toes
- Broken nose
- 4 damaged teeth (1 missing)
- 12 stitches in the cheek
- 9 stitches in the forehead
- Bursitis in elbow
- Bone spur in the elbow
- Hospitalized due to MRSA staph infection in the arm
- Countless ringworm infections
- Cauliflower ear (both ears)

TIMELINE | THE JOURNEY

1995 - Began wrestling

2000 - US High School All-American (7th place)

2005 - First MMA fight (Tijuana, Mexico)

2007 - Won first Championship title

2007 - Signed with *Bodog Fight League*

2008 - Won second MMA Championship title

2009 - Won Third MMA Championship title

2009 - Signed with the WEC

2010 - Won IBJJF Blue Belt Nogi World Championship

2011 - Represented Team U.S.A. in New Zealand

2011 - Occupation: Fighter documentary released

2012 - Had back surgery

2012 - Won IBJJF purple belt Nogi World Championship

2014 - Opened California Mixed Martial Arts

2014 - Bellator debut (the infamous Von Flue choke that made worldwide headlines)

2014 - Won IBJJF brown belt Nogi World Championship

2015 - Won first pro-Jiu-Jitsu tournament (Metamoris Challengers)

2015 - Fight to Win Pro Debut (Won by decision)
2016 - Received Jiu-Jitsu Blackbelt
2016 – EBI Debut (1-1)
2016 – Inducted into the Rancho Cordova Sports Hall of Fame
2017 - EBI Combat Jiu-Jitsu debut (2nd place)
2017 - Combat Jiu-Jitsu World Champion (1st in history)
2018 - IBJJF blackbelt Nogi Worlds (silver medal)
2019 - Retired from the sport of MMA (26 fights, 4 countries, 3 championship titles)
2020 - Fight to Win pro (Won by heel hook)
2021 - Life of a Fighter documentary was released
2022 - Coach IMMAF USA Pan American Team
2023 - Coach IMMAF USA National Team

MMA

3x WEC Veteran
2x Bellator Veteran
3x Championship title holder
Top 10 sportsmanship moments in combat sports history

JIU-JITSU

1st Combat Jiu-Jitsu World Champion
3x IBJJF World Champion
4x SJJIF World Champion
Metamoris Challengers Champion
3x Naga Champion
3x Fight to Win Veteran
2x Ebi Veteran
2nd Degree Blackbelt

FILM

Occupation: Fighter - Documentary
Life of a Fighter - Documentary

ACKNOWLEDGMENTS

Mom and Dad,

Thank you for all your years of support and tough love. Thank you for pushing me to do sports as a kid. You put up with my bullshit and never gave up on me. I hope that I have made you proud.

My sister, Shanna (number 1 fan),

You have been my biggest supporter since day one—right from the start, when you were jumping up and down screaming into the cage, to me coaching you during your first Jiu-Jitsu tournament. I love you.

Monica,

The love of my life, I never knew what that word really meant until I met you. You are the reason I push so hard. I couldn't do any of this without you. Thank you for being my partner in crime and my true ride or die. I can't wait to see the rest of the world with you.

Levi,

You have seen me in my darkest moments. You have also seen me at my brightest. You have never judged me but always have been the one to call me out when I needed it. You even let me get beat up in my first fight because you said that I didn't want you to jump in. Thank you for being the brother I have needed all these years and for always being there when I need you the most.

* * *

Sean Choi,

You changed my life forever. You taught me the lessons of Jiu-Jitsu and took me under your wing when you had no real reason to. I will always be grateful for your guidance and mentorship... even for the days you would smash me into the ground until I quit.

* * *

John Putnam,

You unknowingly sparked the fire in me that led me down this path of self-discovery. I have learned so much from you. Not just in business but in life.

* * *

Carlos Cespedes,

My brother from another mother. It's been an amazing ride. From roommates to Jiu-Jitsu, and now making movies. You have been a monumental helping in the process of becoming who I am today.

* * *

Seb Zewdie,

The impossible Ethiopian, you showed me what it truly means to train like an elite athlete. You pushed me to levels I could have never expected.

Daniel Collins,

Thank you for opening your doors to me and your belief in what we could achieve. This is still just the beginning.

Louie Schwartz,

The black sheep of the gang. You are an inspiration, more than you know. Thank you for your belief in me, your friendship, and, most of all, your dedication to making this world a better place.

Ray Alexander,

The man who never trusts me. Thank you for your passion for martial arts, your belief in my vision, and the writing you helped with to make this book so special.

Josh Barnett,

The Warmaster, thank you for the years of guidance and mentorship that many would not understand. We have been doing this thing for a long time, and I'm honored to share so much of what has happened—and will continue to happen—with you.

* * *

Lyoto Machida,

Thank you for trusting me with not only your students but your training as well. You have been an amazing part of my story and have become family.

Pedro Munhoz,

It has been an honor to ride by your side. We have been across the world together. You inspire me to be not only a better coach but a better friend.

Russell Kairouz,

The Love muscle. You have been by my side since the beginning of this ride. When both of us were completely broke, to now having our amazing families and full blown careers. Thank you for always believing in me. Not going to lie, you should have stuck to TV. "Swim dating with the love muscle". Sounds like a winner.

Fernando Machado,

The Brazilian Gorilla. You moved across the world and have been through so much. Thank you for believing in me. I can't wait the world to see your story.

Michel Valenzuela,

You're one of the only guys who I have ever met that has a work ethic like me. You're a machine. If it wasn't for you during our college days, I would have probably never stayed in LA and never found martial arts.

* * *

Dr. Reed,

Twenty years you have been putting me back together. You are not only the best chiropractor in the world, but you're an amazing friend and mentor.

* * *

Dr. Justin Paquett,

The Dr. who did his own thing when my back was unbearable, you were the only one who thought we could beat this. Much of my success after surgery is credited to the work you did.

* * *

Dr. William Kessler,

Thank you for the years of always being there for the athletes you work with. Most people will never understand what we go through. You are the man.

* * *

Dr. Andrew Schroeder,

The doc of docs, you have opened your office to not only myself but my athletes. I will never be able to thank you enough for the selflessness and generosity you have demonstrated, with zero expectations of receiving anything in return. Your hospitality, kindness, and support will never be forgotten.

* * *

Aissa Juarez,

Thank you for your relentless support through the craziest times in not only my career but also my life. From the days at KROQ, you made me feel like a superstar to the insanity we had at PKG. Take it out of your face.

* * *

Rose Gracie,
You have been in this game longer than most of us. Thank you for believing in me and your passion for making Jiu Jitsu something that everyone should be exposed to.

* * *

TJ Romano,
La Jefa. One day you are going to fire me. Thank you for your relentless belief in me and the vision of the academy. You have defined the definition of what it means to go get it.

* * *

Andre Enzensberger,
The man behind the camera, thank you for creating a story that truly showed the world what it takes to be a fighter. The documentary, Occupation: Fighter changed the game.

* * *

Dom, Chase & Cooper,
My original 3. You guys have held your faith in me for over the last 10 years. I have been honored to ride with you through thick and thin, to call you brothers, and to promote you as my first black belts.

* * *

Cooper,

Not a day goes by that we don't miss you. Please give the guys above a strong strangle for me.

* * *

Logan & Luca

Logan,

My son, the now little Savage. You are and your mother are the key to everything great in this world. You were born into a chaotic and crazy time as the pandemic was at its peak. Your infectious happiness and joy spreads to everyone you come in contact with. I can't wait to watch you grow older, to learn from you and most of all, to see the amazing leader you will be to your younger brother.

* * *

Luca,

As I finished writing this book, your mom and I found out you were coming into our lives. Another addition to the family. Another Savage to the clan. We all can't wait to meet you. Dad, Mom and Logan.

* * *

You,

The reader, thank you for allowing me to share my story. I have had so many incredible moments in my journey, both the highs and lows. But being able to impact at least one person makes me feel as if it was all worth it.

Milton Keynes UK
Ingram Content Group UK Ltd.
UKHW022354310324
440366UK00001B/80